ABOUT THE

I am a BACP accredited counsell‹
of three. I have worked in the pe
life, including many years with special needs children in schools.
As a counsellor I have worked with persons struggling with
issues including addictions, anxieties, obsessions and many
others.

I have researched and written numerous health articles for my
local newspaper, *The Newbury Weekly News,* some parts of which I
have used in this book

J. M. Ascroft-Leigh MBACP Accredited
Counsellor/Psychotherapist
UKRCP Registered

COUNSELLING D I Y

Understanding Mental Health

J. M. Ascroft-Leigh

Published 2011 by arima publishing
www.arimapublishing.com

ISBN 978 1 84549 515 2

Printed and bound in the United Kingdom

Typeset in Garamond 12/14

Swirl is an imprint of arima publishing.

arima publishing
ASK House, Northgate Avenue
Bury St Edmunds, Suffolk IP32 6BB
t: (+44) 01284 700321
www.arimapublishing.com

DEDICATION

To Philomena
who, in spite of her handicap, spoke to me with her soul

ABOUT THE BOOK

This book gives the reader an opportunity for self therapy and to look at themselves, how they grew up and how circumstances influenced the way they are now. It outlines broadly what is needed to live a healthy and productive life, and how they can achieve a better understanding of their perception of it.

The book demystifies some of the more complicated concepts of psychology and makes them more user-friendly.

It is not for the faint hearted, and deals with hard facts about mental disturbances and mental disorders, not to frighten the reader, but as a reality check.

J. M. Ascroft-Leigh

CONTENTS

SECTION ONE

SECTION TWO

SECTION ONE

Chapter ONE
TAKING STOCK –What is mental health?

Mental Health Check

In order to know whether we have a problem, we first need to understand what we are aiming for. To understand mental disturbance, we need to know what mental health is. It is therefore useful to review how things started with you.

When you were born you were already a very clever person. A long evolutional process provided you with a birth package whereby you already had the capacity to know what you needed for survival. You knew you needed your mother for food and trusted her to provide you with that. You knew you needed warmth and comfort. You were pre-programmed to know how to summon help to get your needs met in order to survive and thrive. Mother had her instinctive radar on to respond. You were in a symbiotic relationship. She and your father went to great lengths to protect you from harm. That's evolutional.

Equally, as well as knowing what you needed, you also instinctively knew what you didn't need. If you were cold or accidentally pricked with a nappy pin you will have cried and shown distress and summoned your primary carer for help. Therefore, nature makes it quite easy for parents.

Mum, dad and little me

Technically, compared to most other animals human babies are born very early and could certainly benefit from a longer gestation period. However, because the brain is already quite large at birth and will grow 2.6 times larger during the first 12 months and its body will be three times as heavy in the first year, it would mean re-designing the shape of a woman's body quite drastically to accommodate such a shape and size. [1] Nature, therefore, includes in the birth package a convenient and temporary pre-programmed set of behaviours. We sometimes call this instinct.

A baby is born to two parents; a man and a woman. That's for a good reason. Baby needs both sexes around to study. By the age of two he will have worked out what sex he is and will identify with his same sex parent for learning his craft; that is, how to behave according to his gender. This is a wonderful time for baby and given the right environment he will learn and develop to reach his maximum potential for good health, both physically and mentally. He will have his conscious and unconscious beady eye on his favourite role model and internalise whatever skills he can absorb and practice for his gender training. His opposite sex parent will be his reflective sexual role model and will give him a base on which to model femaleness in his head for seeking a mate in the future. For the next five years he will absorb everything they say and do, and root it in his psyche as his base learning. This is a chair – this is what grass feels like - this is what you eat and say - and this is how you go to the toilet. Baby learns how to become a member of his social group. If baby's brain is the software then his parents are the hardware who will program his biological computer.

The difference between your pc and this biological bit of genius is that certainly by the time he is approximately age five, something amazing has happened and his clever little mind starts to make sense of what he has learned. He learns to think. He will then feel the hot radiator and say, "ouch – mummy was right, it does hurt when I touch it" but he will also say, "daddy was wrong; my teeth did not fall out when I ate that whole bag of sweets". It is the emergence of a fragile ego. The ego is the mature self.

We have all heard of Sigmund Freud's id, ego and superego.[2] The id, technically the German word for 'I' is the instinctual demands that have got mother's attention when he screamed for his breast milk, and is the line of communication he uses to get his needs met. He is only tiny so it needs to be powerful. The superego is the parent programming; the 25,000 hours of input which his brain has absorbed from the information we have passed on to him so far, in his short five years of life. The all important ego is the sense of self; developed as a result of these two influences in relation to his world. The ego, in time, becomes the mature self. This is the space to watch because from here on in it is a contest between these three forces to see who wins. In there lies the secret of mental health.

As children, we don't question our parents. Our minds and bodies just react to their commands. "Yes, I will put my bike away" or "No, I don't want to eat this brussel sprout". If the atmosphere that parents provide is good for baby's needs, then baby's body and mind will grow and thrive. If the atmosphere causes baby anxiety, such as shouting at baby, or parents shouting at each other, baby will know that is not good for him and react. For his own good, baby is the perfect parasite. Baby is still programmed to protect itself from harm, and parents are the back-up. If they are mature, they will also want to protect him from harm. This is the simple reason why some people will harm children or each other. It is either to protect themselves, or because they are not mature themselves.

So now, within these healthy parameters, a child will thrive, mentally and physically, or more correctly, neurologically, psychologically and physiologically. In order to protect him, he needs boundaries to keep him safe, such as a fence to keep him from running into the road. He needs a firm 'no' if there is broken glass nearby. He needs rest when he is tired to restore his energy. He also needs regular healthy meals which help his body grow and fuel his little engine. Baby then needs an atmosphere for learning in order to stimulate neurological development, which means his little brain is free to soak up all the things going on around him.

He has been issued with carers to protect him from danger, and to soothe him if danger cannot be avoided. If, for example he loses sight of mummy in a shopping mall and becomes distressed she will soon re-assure him that she is close by and watching over him. He is reminded that he still needs her for protection and logs that in his memory bank.

Who am I?

As he grows and begins to separate from his parents, he will begin to see himself as an individual. He has a built in sense of wanting and needing to be treated with respect. All his life-building chemicals will react favourably to being treated respectfully. For example, if he is treated by his parent mechanically, as an object and not as an individual, there may be a constant low-level anxiety. He will eventually get used to the way he is treated but psychologically he may have a life-long yearning for affirmation, and never fully understand why that is. His confidence will be affected. It is therefore important that he is acknowledged respectfully and treated with regard.

Alternatively, if his parent becomes servile and lets baby take full charge of their relationship, he will also have problems. If mum is anxious every time baby summons help then baby will soon sense that anxiety and feel unsafe. He will then feel insecure and cry even more. It is unsettling for him to have so much power over mum and he will feel disturbed and insecure. If his boundaries are not firmly reinforced by his parents he will be very angry with mum and dad and flounder as he will not have a clear idea of what he can and cannot do. For example, if a baby was left in the middle of Wembley stadium he will feel unsettled as he cannot see boundaries which he needs as reference points to log into his memory. For the same reason he also needs emotional boundaries. He needs to know mum will reliably keep him warm and safe and be there for him. Mum needs to confidently take charge of baby and of what is in baby's best interest.

In this atmosphere, a child can thrive and is on track to become a mentally healthy adult. His chemical make-up is in harmony with his inevitable and vital growth. There is homeostasis.

Those little grey cells

Before birth, the foetal brain is unravelling and expanding. It is growing 250,000 neurons per minute.[3] This unwrapping of the convoluted tissue in the outer cortex is triggered by a genetic process and is changing it into an organ which will eventually be able to take control of itself.

After birth it begins a second explosive phase of development which is stimulated not only by its genetic programming but also by its external new world. It is therefore important not to interfere with this and provide an environment which lets nature do its stuff. The new brain, a dense forest of interconnecting nerve cells responds to sensory messages like sound, smell and touch. It constantly unravels and updates as it grows and begins its process of adapting to its environment and heads towards maturity. If baby sits on the floor and there is a red ball some metres away, then it is the act of wanting to experience and touch that ball which will cause baby to move towards it. This act will stimulate a frenzy of neurological growth.

60% of a baby's food intake goes into providing the energy needed for brain development.[4] It therefore makes sense to give baby as much as he needs and the best quality food you can provide. Again, nature makes it easy for us and mum is already carrying a perfect balance of nutritious food in her breasts.

Computer update

With these physical conditions met, for mental health a young child watches members of his social group for guidance. He will seek out his same sex parent as his preferred role model.

Their little biological computers are incorporating this new information and constantly categorising and updating and filing. Because they are human computers, they will also try to make sense of what they are learning, and soon start to include ideas into their programming. Just like it is with our vision, we see flat surfaces with each eye, but with both eyes we have three dimensional vision. If you put a hand over one eye, you will see a flat scene. You can determine depth by the size of things. If a car is small it is farther away then if it is larger. Remove your hand and you will become aware that you have depth perception. So it is with the developmental brain. With its input, we create ideas and we are therefore, more then the sum of our parts.

Not only is a child influenced by his surroundings, but he also begins to make conscious and unconscious choices to shape his mental development, as he adapts to his environment. We have only recently learned that a brand new baby is cleverer then a one year old.[5] He is born with skills he quickly looses. Neurologists now tell us that from the moment we are born, we begin shedding neurons that are not needed as we begin our adaptation process to fit into our social and environmental world. Quite simply, what isn't used withers and dies. What is used develops. This is why we all thrive in all climates and all social groups. We prune to fit. Now it gets really interesting as that is the basis of social deviancies as well. Fetishes and obsessions, even addictions, are often the result of the adaptive processes gone awry. (See Section 2, Fetishes and OC Behaviour)

So now he is watching and learning. He is internalising behaviour. He watches daddy nailing some wood. He has seen Bob the builder do this on television and he knows boys become men, and men build things. "Daddy, can I have a go?" Daddy gives him a plastic hammer and nails and off he goes. He is having an experience of manly or gender-specific behaviour to plug into his computer, strengthening his earlier experience of watching Bob the Builder and includes the sounds and smells of father's work, including father's mannerisms and mood. At the same time his is internalising a multitude of other associated stimulants, such as the smell of mum's soup and the tapping of the rain on the garage window. If he feels happy then he will forever associate these conditions with happiness. His computer is constantly updating and upgrading all this information. If these influences are also conducive to the larger, social group, then he is still on track for mentally healthy development.

Learning coping strategies to deal with anxiety

One day, our 3 year old runs into the garden, trips on some stones and cuts his knee. He bleeds. He will feel the pain. He will look down and see the blood and scream in horror summoning help. With his limited knowledge, he will likely think all his blood will leak out and that he will die. His mother comes running, comforts him, mops up the blood and assures him he will be all right. His anxiety level will have been high. His body would have prepared him for danger, but danger has been dissipated, and his chemical levels will return to normal. His mother has demonstrated support, comfort and new information to help him. He has logged that as well. He will internalise that *strategy* for coping with falling, and after a few more of these types of incidents, he will have internalised the very important skill of being soothed, and of soothing. Having computed that strategy he will eventually know how to self-soothe and how to soothe others. He has internalised a life skill.

As he grows up in a healthy, mature environment he will learn many such coping strategies until he reaches adulthood and he is able to stand alone, and later support those who need him.

What happens if I have a problem and don't have a coping strategy?

When Jake came to visit Sam with his mum, the ladies had wine in the kitchen and he and Jake played outside. Jake was strong and took Sam's new tricycle and when Sam felt very upset because he couldn't play with his own, new tricycle Sam cried but mother didn't hear. He then went indoors and played alone with his Lego. Outside he had felt anxious and unhappy and as no help came to protect him from the harm of anxiety, he retreated. As there was no one to teach him a strategy to help him cope, he used his natural instinct to protect himself from harm and began to incorporate an ego defence. He disavowed and pretended his friend was not there.

Ego defences are what we instinctively use to protect ourselves from anxiety if we have no learned coping strategy. For mental health our ego, the mature self, the part of us which has learned how to be a healthy, useful member of a social group not only uses the coping strategies it has learned, but can fill in the gaps by employing ego defences. Children who do not learn appropriate coping strategies will have to make them up with their immature and underdeveloped psyches. They may pick up inappropriate strategies from friends, or films, or public role models. Failing that, they will employ unconscious ways of dealing with impending anxiety and use ego defences.

What are Ego Defences?

As a species, we are very resilient. From the moment we start our day, we try to organise our lives to keep anxiety to a minimum. Too much anxiety is a killer, and will start to break down our mental and physical health, if it is not dealt with. For example, if we don't have much time to get ready to go to work in the morning, to prevent the anxiety caused by rushing, we might get our clothes and things ready the night before. If the boss wants that report on his desk first thing Monday morning, we may do extra work on the w/e to prevent trouble. If we are obsessive, we may work every evening to get it absolutely perfect.

If we are worriers and struggle with invading thoughts in the evening, we may have an extra glass of wine after dinner. If it is easier for us to shout at our children rather then take the time to help them work out their problems, we may feel guilty and tuck into an extra helping of mashed potatoes or chocolate mouse to make ourselves feel better.

We use our learned coping defence system to help us keep anxiety at bay. However, if we find ourselves in a predicament where we don't know how to cope we may use our psychological back-up system and unconsciously employ an ego defence, a strategy our automatic protection system comes up with to protect us from the immediate harm of anxiety.

These can be a little or a lot irrational, and sometimes difficult to detect. If we are not protected from harm, while our brains are still developing, and if we have not been taught by our social group or parents how to deal with certain problems, our psyches kick in and do it for us. If these are rooted in our brains during our early years, they hard-wire and are then more difficult to change; difficult but not impossible. For example, if Sam is often left to cope with bullies and not taught how to protect himself, he may employ his own instinctive way again, and grow up learning to avoid conflict by pretending it isn't there. Denial or disavowal will be his ego defence. That will give him problems in adulthood.

A more serious example of denial is if a girl looses her mother who dies when she is ten years old. That will be very traumatic for her and without proper support she may pretend it hasn't happened and refuse to talk about it. She may avoid dealing with her new situation particularly if no one explains to her that it is not her fault, or because of anything she has done. A child who looses a parent feels bereft, and often feels it is somehow their fault. To repair the damage of such psychological trauma, she needs to be allowed to grieve her mother's death, by gently allowing her to face her pain. With help she can internalise a perception of her mother's love and good sense, and then slowly learn to access the memory of her mum when she needs emotional support. It would then also be beneficial for her to find substitutions to fill the gap of a maternal role model as she goes through her teenage years. With this kind of help she will be able to deal with the enormous psychological interruption in her life, and deal with the trauma which may have threatened her mental health.

Another example of an ego defence is if a small child lives in an atmosphere where parents argue a lot he may feel frightened and out of control. Because he cannot control them, and in order to have some sort of control over his world he may want to employ an ego defence. He may line up his little toy soldiers, his stuffed animals and make sure the drawers are all closed. When he wakes up it gives him some comfort to know that his world is in order and his soldiers are just where he left them. If he is good boy maybe his angry parents will stop being angry. He may develop obsessive compulsive behaviours which will neurologically hard-wire in his brain until they feel normal to him. This way he has some control in his perceived dangerous world which was threatened by the fearful noises made by his caretakers, the two people his life depends on.

Another example of an ego defence is that of 'acting out'. When two siblings are arguing over a toy and no one demonstrates to them how to maturely resolve the conflict they will either fight to resolve or intimidate and bully to win the coveted toy. For parents it is a perfect opportunity to show children how to deal with conflict. It is no good just taking the toy away from them, to save yourself the bother, but to use this as an opportunity to demonstrate a fair way for them to learn to deal with conflict; a useful coping strategy.

It is for these reasons that it is vital that children are protected from the harm anxiety can do, until they are older. There is sufficient anxiety in their young world to give them practice and experience in small doses. If harm can not be avoided, then they need to be supported by their loved ones, and shown ways of dealing with the anxiety that problems may have caused. By passing on to our children the coping strategies we have learned from our parents, and adjusting them to adhere to modern thinking, we can help our children live more productively, so that they can enjoy their lives with greater contentment. Then as adults they can live full and productive lives and not be hindered by their need to protect themselves from things that make them anxious. Ego defences should be a last resort for coping with anxiety, as these can be irrational and more difficult to understand, and most certainly more difficult to unlearn if these then become a problem.

Some common ego defences are

a) <u>Denial,</u> used when a person refuses to face the reality of a situation, such as, "I don't have a father", or "She's not gone, just wait and see. She'll be back really soon". Also, a person who dresses very young may be in denial of growing older.

b) <u>Regression</u> – behaving in a child-like manner in order to avoid coping or dealing with a situation which is too stressful.

c) <u>Displacement</u> – releasing hostility onto the nearest, non-threatening target, sometimes called 'kick-the-dog' syndrome. So that, if the boss admonishes you, you shout at your wife, who takes it out on the child, who kicks the dog.

d) <u>Reaction-Formation</u> – conceals real feelings by saying things like, "I didn't want that job anyway" or "I don't care what you do – just please yourself". These could ward off feelings of rejection or abandonment.

e) <u>Repression</u> – feelings or emotions which are pushed into the unconscious as a base on which other defences are built. For example if a child has been abused by a parent they may have buried the experience out of consciousness because it is too stressful and because they need the parent.

f) <u>Projection</u> – when someone feels such frightening feelings about themselves, that it is easier to assume that someone else is harbouring such feelings towards him. Or blaming others for your mistakes, and transferring guilt. "If you hadn't put that rug there I wouldn't have tripped over it, and hurt myself."

g) <u>Rationalisation</u> - inventing reasons to explain behaviour, "I'm fat because of a glandular problem, not from eating". "He didn't want to go out with me because it was too far to travel".

h)   <u>Introjection</u> – absorbing parental values to avoid making your own decisions, or to adopt the values of 'the crowd' as a survival tactic.

i)   <u>Sublimation</u> – constructive channelling of aggressive or other misplaced feelings into something like sport, art, or exercising, etc.

j)   <u>Compensation</u> – can also be constructive – people who are lacking in one area can make it up by being good at something else thus getting their share of social credence. If you are very good at science your dad might forgive you for not making the football team.   A negative use of compensation is when parents use pressure on children to fulfil their lost dreams.   This is especially not good if a child has to deny his own dreams.

Ego defences will kick in if we don't have learned coping strategies, in order to protect us from anxiety.

I need to feel valued

As well as protecting ourselves from anxiety, we need to feel valued. We use much energy in our day to bank up credibility or kudos with our peers. When we are in credit it can buffer us in case we loose points when we are caught off guard. *For mental health we all need to be a valued member of our social group.* We feel misery and low self-esteem if we feel that no one likes us.

So if the boss suddenly shouts our name from his office for all to hear, we certainly hope that the joke we told at the office party last week got enough laughs to protect our self-esteem from this event. Then we are able to make light of it at lunch unless our red, puffy eyes give us away. Be sure to understand, it would be a hugely insensitive boss who would use such a display of public humiliation.

The two greatest rewards

Having internalised sufficient coping strategies to deal with his day to day life, and having his parents nearby and accessible for support, our hero is still on track to maintain mental health and thereby leave him powering full steam ahead to reach his fullest potential.

In life, we need reward for effort. Much of Western society subscribes and often exploits this human frailty and much energy is spent proffering and seeking rewards. For a child, parents often believe that a toy or a chocolate sweet will be a great reward; however, a child's most desired reward is parental approval. If a child feels valued by his parents he will value himself, and this will give him a healthy self-concept.

If our growing hero has brothers and sisters, we also need to see if he has learned how to manage his life with these competitors for that all important reward, parental approval. The two most notable and often unappreciated aspects of being a child are

a)   his ability to adapt, and

b)   his desire to please his primary carers.

We must never underestimate these two powerful motivators. *Adapting* will give him an unconscious reward by becoming intrinsic, and thereby reducing anxiety; and *pleasing his primary carers* gives him the reward of acceptance which he needs to assure him that evolutionally his development is on track, as he knows innately that his parents want the best for him.

Who's in charge?

As ever, if he is to maintain mental health, there needs to be a reasonable amount of control over his environment so that it does not overwhelm him. Although they no longer need to be as vigilant as new parents because children now use language to communicate with them, parents still feature as important figures for growing children. As they are still learning coping strategies to arm them for life, having brothers and sisters helps them early on to learn negotiation skills within a group. As it then 'sets' in the grey matter it becomes a part of their shaping. Mature parents will help children learn these skills by demonstrating fairness both by example and action. If parents struggle with their own coping skills and a child learns to get his way by bullying, or crying or cheating, these inappropriate ways will 'set' in his brain and will be his way of dealing with things in his adult world. Because parents were unhelpful in teaching him mature strategies and cooperative skills, then in order to protect himself from the anxiety that accompany such poor skills, he may cause harm in the form of anxiety to his brothers and sisters. "Mum, Matthew took my toy". Mature parents will teach appropriate ways of dealing with younger and older siblings, and encourage their children by teaching and demonstrating skills which will protect them and still be conducive to the larger group. This way parents know that they are doing their best to move their children maturely towards independence.

This is an exercise to help understand what goes on between parents and children.

As a parent, if two of your children are squabbling over a toy, how would you handle that? Options are:

i. *Stop fighting, you are giving me a headache*

ii. *Stop fighting and go to your rooms*

iii. *If you can't agree then I'll take the toy away*

iv. *Right. What's going on? Take it in turns to tell me what's happening and we can try to agree how to solve this problem.*

Option i. <u>Stop fighting – you are giving me a headache</u>

You are presenting yourself to your children as helpless. You are giving them the task of making life easy for you without using the opportunity to show them how to solve a difference of opinion. They are made to feel guilty in that they are responsible for causing their parent pain.

Option ii. <u>Stop fighting and go to your rooms</u>

You are presenting yourself as an autocrat. You have shown them you cannot cope with conflict. You are a ruler who will not tolerate conflict. You are training them to avoid conflict by running away from problems.

Option iii. <u>If you cannot agree then I'll take the toy away</u>

You are punishing them both for not being mature. However, they are children. They are trying to work out how to negotiate, and now there is no opportunity for learning, and MAYBE you have not noticed how Sally is bullying Jake. They now have unprocessed emotions which include anger, pain, frustration, and guilt.

Option iv. <u>Take it in turns to tell me what's happening and we can agree how to solve this problem</u>

This is obviously the mature result. From the time they are born it is your job to nudge them towards independence, and this is yet another social skill they need to learn. Even if one child gets the coveted toy, they will both feel heard and know that they have been treated fairly, and will use that skill in future situations.

Look out school, here I come

Soon our little heroes will be ready for school. For the next thirteen years or so this will be their new, bigger family. Here they will have their coping strategies reinforced and learn plenty of new ones. If they have a healthy foundation for their learning and the new teaching is consistent with what they learned at home, they will go from strength to strength. If the rules are a little different they will simply adapt and slip quickly and effortlessly into both their home world and their school world with ease. For example children may speak a different language and have cultural rituals at home but at school will adopt the language and rules of the school. They will then even re-adapt these to fit in with their social group and use for example the jargon or colloquialisms which are used by their friends. As long as they feel they have value among their social group and have the approval of their parents, they will thrive. Our children are still on track for mental health.

If a growing child does not have to spend the bulk of his energy protecting himself from anxiety, his energy is then naturally spent on learning what life has to teach him. All living things will strive to move in a constructive direction. If the need to reduce anxiety is greater then the desire to move forward then problems arise and comfort will be sought elsewhere.

And now, the end is near…..
Well, here he is. Our little chap is now 'en route' to becoming a young person. He has learned his tables and his geography. He knows what third world countries are and understands about different cultures. He knows that William Shakespeare and Leonardo De Vinci are measures of excellence and that freedom is our right and worth fighting for. He has learned how to behave in public and knows the difference between right and wrong. He has been socialised.

As they approach the end of their secondary school life and the end of their developing years, with the respect and support of their parents and teachers, they will slowly have started to take charge of their own lives. With support they will start to make decisions about their future, venture out into the greater world and soon stand on their own two feet. Nature needs it to be this way, as by then the parents will be getting older and although still able to offer support from a distance, will reach the point where they are no longer able to care for their children. The children will need to care for themselves, and eventually, their future offspring.

In terms of psychological development, he is now a mature adult. He has learned to control his impulses. If he is mentally healthy, he has learned to make informed decisions so that he is not guided by guilt or greed. He does not fear his future and is ready to embrace it with trust and knowledge.

Got it, Mr. Sigmund Freud

There is a healthy balance between his id, his ego and his super-ego, or colloquially, his 'I want', 'I can' and 'I should'. He has learned to control his impulses so that they work for him.

If id, ego and superego are standing in front of a cake shop window, id will say "I want that chocolate cake and I want to gobble it all up right now." Super-ego will say "You should not have it as it is full of fat, sugars and unacceptable cholesterols." However, the ego will say "Yes, we can buy that cake and we will have one piece today and another piece tomorrow." The mature ego will manage the impulsive id and the punitive super-ego.

He will be able to manage his anxiety without needing to *over* indulge in eating, drinking or using opiates in order to cope. **(id).**

He will have enough self-esteem so that he is not intimidated or manipulated by others. (**super-ego)**

He will feel secure within his social group. He will have an understanding of human nature and know that he can tolerate others and their shortcomings, but be able to protect himself and his dependents from the extremes of society. **(ego)**

The ego has landed. Mature behaviour is defined by behaving in a way that is helpful to the self, conducive to personal growth, and contributes to the well-being of the group. It should not be at the expense of the self, the group, or members of the group. For example, if you inadvertently bump into someone, you have made a misjudgement, however if you deliberately bump into them, then you are causing harm to others. If you speak to someone and use language to hurt or discredit him and you have done it unintentionally, then you may be forgiven, however if it is done in order to make yourself look good, then you are causing harm. Environmentally, if you step on an ant without realising that you did, then you are okay, however, if you deliberately step on an ant for no reason other then to kill it, then you are causing harm.

A mature person behaves in a way that enhances his own well being with consideration to his environment which serves him and his community and which gives him value as a member of his social group.

This chapter gives us an idea of what is needed for mental health. The brain is a magnificent and resilient organ and just as it can learn a second language with a different part of the brain, so too, can it modify and relearn new habits, simply by retraining and reprogramming.

Chapter TWO
WHAT'S MY PROBLEM?

Identifying problems

Perhaps you are very clear about what problem or problems you are struggling with. Maybe it is not so clear, however there is a general feeling of discomfort; a strong notion that something is not right. It is then important to identify the feeling or at least, the symptoms.

Do you feel angry, frustrated or depressed? Is there a general feeling of unsettledness invading your life? Do you struggle with loss of confidence or what is referred to as low self-esteem? Are you feeling constantly run down, tired, lethargic? There are a myriad of psychological disturbances that can put a strain on a person's mental and physical health. If mental disturbances are not resolved they very often somatise and your body may start to present with physical symptoms.

Your first port of call is your GP. If he cannot find any underlying causes of your discomfort or suggests it is as a result of emotional issues, it may be time to consider what your body might be trying to tell you.

We all want to wake up in the morning, with that old-fashioned 'glad to be alive' feeling, and leap out of bed, eager to get the day underway. When exactly was the last time you felt like that? If it is hard to remember, then perhaps we can assume that the responsibilities of life are just keeping you slightly tense with a constant level of low anxiety while you juggle your complicated life and try to keep on top of things. For mental health we need a balance of periods of low to zero anxiety to offset the wear and tear on the body during times of high anxiety. We all know we need breaks at weekends and holidays to re-charge the batteries. That's how our western society works and generally, people know how to pace themselves.

Problems with others

For some of us, it is not so simple. For example, if we can not escape anxiety and it is with us all the time, then we have a problem. If a family member who is there all the time causes you anxiety, you have no means of escape. If a partner makes you feel undervalued then it can be hard. If you are a full time carer and resent the caring then you have a problem. If you have depression with little or no support, you have a problem. If you are agoraphobic with little or no support, you have a problem. If you dread going in to work because your boss or colleagues are a constant source of anxiety to you, then life is hard. Therefore, if the situation is such that you have no way of protecting yourself from the anxiety it causes then you have a problem. These problems can slowly begin to erode your physical health, and stress-related illnesses can begin to surface.

Problems with yourself

Are you the problem? Do you feel there is something fundamentally wrong with you? Do you feel your personality is not up to scratch and it feels that other people have a problem with you? Do you feel judged, disapproved of, criticised? Do you feel all these things always, or some of these things sometimes, but certainly more often then feels comfortable? Has your self-confidence taken a nose dive?

Problems with addictions

Perhaps some 'thing' is creating unmanageable anxiety for you, such as too much drinking, or smoking. Maybe computer or internet gambling, or gaming have got a hold of you and you are struggling with controlling these compulsions. Maybe eating too much or too little, or binging or purging food has you in its grip.

Problems with impulses

Perhaps things are a little more serious and you struggle with secrets. Do you have anti-social impulses which you are reluctant to share with others for fear of being ridiculed or exposed? Perhaps you are cutting your arms or parts of your body to release stress. Maybe you are addicted to sex, or have unusual sexual impulses, or sexual fantasies or other fantasies you are reluctant to share, even with your closest family members for fear of ridicule or exposure. Maybe impulsive thoughts invade your mind or you think you have a deep psychological disturbance.

Maybe you have unhealthy sexual attractions and worry about how much you can trust yourself with these, as they have the potential to harm others.

Some problems can become overwhelming and begin to rule our lives. Healthy pre-occupations should take up a normal part of our lives. If things begin to feel abnormal, then they may become the greater focus of our lives and begin to dominate us. It then stops healthy progression. For example, if sex in a relationship is not a problem it fits snugly into a normal routine and is a healthy part of a couple's life. If, however, sex is a problem, then it becomes about 90% of the focus. It is the same with other areas of our lives. If something becomes a problem, then it features as a major focus and becomes disproportionate to all other problems.

Problems with work-related stress

Sometimes the responsibilities at work are very consuming and it is difficult to switch off when you go home. It is hard to put the ropes down and become the other person you need to be which is father, mother, husband, wife, partner, brother or sister. It takes a great deal of mental energy to release your brain from work thoughts and 'go domestic'. The idea of waking up in the morning and wondering if you will remember to pick up all the different strands again is worrying and difficult. It is hard to let go of all the ropes and sometimes there will be some residual rope clutching while you try to feed baby her carrot mash and help little Jenni with her spelling. It is difficult to keep your two worlds apart and sometimes they enmesh. It is difficult when you are holding on to some important thoughts about tomorrow's meeting while your wife is explaining that the dishwasher is leaving the glasses cloudy again.

Negative Thinking: We are sometimes our own worst enemies

If we are good at something, and we have been given a diploma or degree, or a good wage to reinforce that, it gives us social credibility and we have extra confidence in what we do. This makes us feel valuable in our social group and gives us respect. That's healthy. That is a natural process and we can confirm that by noticing that our bodies react to it favourably by all the life enhancing chemicals that are being produced in our system. The dopamine and other neurotransmitters our body produces when we feel good about ourselves enhances the immune system, makes us feel good, and promotes other areas of good health. That is proof. When we do well we can feel good. There is a comprehensive match between who we are and how we think others see us. We are then useful to our social group and want to be a part of it. We may then even have surplus energy to help others, etc. We are then content, happy and healthy, and a functioning member of our society.

Unfortunately, our sometimes fickle and capricious society often lets us feel the opposite. We are often made to feel unworthy. We can easily collude with this process by telling ourselves we have little or low value or allowing others to make us feel unworthy. In fact, there are many people who actively choose to make us feel bad so that it makes them look good by comparison and can boost their egos at our expense. We cannot really stop them if it is an ego defence they learned in childhood as perhaps they did not learn adequate coping strategies to become sociable members of their group. But we can stop ourselves from letting it affect us.

If for example if someone has learned inadvertently as a child that in order to feel good you need to put someone down, then that is how they will behave as for them it became a learned coping strategy for life. "Don't worry, darling – they are a family of complainers. Of course you never meant to take their bike".

Alternatively, if children were bullied and were often made to feel inadequate by, for example, an older brother or sister and if parents did not help, then being angry with others and discrediting them to make them look bad will be an ego defence. It then becomes the only way that person can protect himself from the anxiety of being bullied. It is what he needs to do to feel better. "I hate you, bro, and everybody hates you!" He knows deep down it isn't right but unless he recognises his anti-social habits, it will be difficult for him to change that behaviour. It is therefore important to recognise why you feel bad as a result of someone else's behaviour. You have the option to take charge of that. Like the cliché – it's their problem, not yours.

Maybe I am rubbish

We don't need coaching to have negative thoughts. This is universal. If you use self-sabotage as a way of getting through your day then you have a problem. We really are sometimes our own worst enemies. Negative thinking is damaging and training yourself to reinforce negative thinking by programming your brain this way can make things worse. Sustained negative programming becomes hard-wired and is difficult to shift unless you become aware of it and actively change it. We will believe and reinforce whatever is our perception of ourselves. If someone continually tells you that you are stupid then eventually you may start to believe it and take on that programming yourself. "I am so stupid".

Change is possible. The current thinking about changing behaviour is that it takes anywhere from 3 weeks to 3 months plus to change behaviour. For example, if you move your cutlery into a different drawer in the kitchen it takes about 3 weeks to get used to the new system. This is of course age dependent and a young mind will adapt faster then an older person, however, it takes time for any brain to take on the new regime. It then goes into the 'automatic pilot' part of the brain and joins the vast arena of automatic activities that we take for granted. Some of these include skipping down the stairs, running, kicking a stone down the path, co-ordinating hand and eye when eating or writing, as well as the more complicated learned skills of driving a car, typing a letter or playing piano. Playing piano is a behaviour change that takes years to learn and is at the opposite end of the spectrum of changing the cutlery drawer. It is however a lovely example of complex adjustments our brain is capable of, given direction, perseverance and the right conditions. We all marvel at a superb piano concerto.

The brain is not unlike your computer, and is in fact the most sophisticated of computers, as it can self generate ideas from the information given. Therefore if we have a negative idea about ourselves, such as for example "I am boring" and we reinforce that idea over and over, our brain will adapt to the new regime and incorporate all the other information it has around that and eventually hard-wire it into the automatic pilot part of our programming. You can see how debilitating that would be for you. You have then self-sabotaged and confined your own personality to that of being boring. That will then be accompanied by a sustained level of anxiety every time you are with others. After all, you are responsible for boring all those lovely people in the room.

Young people are particularly vulnerable to such suggestions. They have a big need to be accepted, first by their parents and then by their peers. If a young person is unfortunate enough to be in an environment where there are many who feed their own egos at the expense of others, and they have not got the self-confidence or life skills to withstand that, then they will be harmed. It will then take much hard work to rebuild their ego back to health. It will be difficult to stand shoulder to shoulder with others as an equal.

Homeostasis

It is therefore preferable that we are nurtured towards a strong and healthy self-concept. This is not just a case of choosing to program a brain with whatever we would like it to do, but more a tuning in to what it needs to maximise mental health. It knows what it needs and will respond favourably to the programming that is conducive to supporting a healthy self-concept. A healthy mind will seek homeostasis which is when body and mind are content and the chemicals produced result in physical and mental health. It is then in a position to thrive and strive.

For example, if you always wanted to be an airline pilot, and then became one, you will feel right. If, however, you have always wanted to be an airline pilot and ended up as a bank employee there will be unsettledness. Neither profession is wrong but your perception of it is wrong. If you, then, do not come to terms with that, it may, over time, begin to erode your health.

A healthy self-concept comes from being raised in an environment where particular criteria for mental health have been met. These include those things like *unconditional love* so that self-respect is nurtured and consequently a respect for all things that support the life of our world. We need *protection from harm*, so that the seeds for anxiety do not get rooted at a time when we are too helpless to deal with it. This means as children we need to be protected from adult problems. We need to learn in small, age appropriate doses, how to solve problems and be recognised and appreciated for having done that. We need to be protected from adult anxiety because when given a problem which is bigger then a solution that we can comprehend, we will be anxious and not ready for that. That means when a little boy makes a gun out of a stick so that he can quite naturally protect his world, he does not need to hear that it is wrong and that he is suddenly responsible for all the evil in the world. It will log into his psyche as anxiety and if he has no strategy to cope with that, then his body will use the back-up system of an ego defence to give him the comfort he needs which may become an inappropriate life skill for our future. He can hear of the destructiveness of war when he is older and ready to see the global implications of it.

He needs to learn, in small appropriate steps how to do things for himself, when he is ready so that one day he will be able to become independent, and a useful member of his social group.

We learn how to be mature from our families

If we have seen our family dealing with problems calmly and responsibly then a sense of that will root in our psyche and when we are older and problems appear we will not feel anxious or misery. We will know how to deal with these appropriately. We need careful and individual training to get it right and to get it wrong. We need the experience of getting it right and see how that feels as well as how the praise feels. We then learn eventually to take charge of our own lives.

We also need to make mistakes without judgement as we will be our own worst critic, and so that we will have the experience of feeling failure as well. Having the experience of getting things wrong and figuring out how to put them right is as important as all our other learning experiences so that we can log that and not be frightened in the future by that. When we are adults we will occasionally get things wrong and we will need to know how to handle that with colleagues and bosses and family members.

This is life skills training. If we learn problem solving at home and are rewarded with parent approval, we will have a deep and natural sense of self worth. If someone then challenges us, we will quite naturally defend ourselves and not be harmed by that. We will have respect for ourselves and for others.

The damage of early anxiety

An example of great stress causing children anxiety at school these days are the Sats tests. These tests are designed to monitor whether teachers are teaching appropriately and to see if they have covered the required syllabus. It is to check and see if children have been taught what they should have been taught and that nationally the general population of children have absorbed the learning. As a bi-product these tests can show and measure a child's skills and capabilities. Good and possibly useful information. Children can not prepare for general knowledge tests. Unfortunately, many schools advise children of these tests which means children will worry. Knowing about them in advance can create a competitive atmosphere, and will undoubtedly cause humiliation and intimidation and anxiety for children. To be useful without doing harm, these tests need to be presented without prior knowledge and just as a school activity.

Children have no method of protecting themselves and are often pressurised by parents to perform well at these. There is no way to prepare themselves as their aptitudes are being measured, so the only thing they can do is worry. They are thus unwittingly issued with the task of making both parents and teachers look good. Such problems can leave a lasting and devastating effect on children as those adults they trusted gave them an impossible task, presented with high expectations which caused them anxiety. That kind of anxiety rooted will rear its ugly head throughout their lives and may induce panic attacks for those who already are plagued with such expectations as a matter of course.

Reprogramming Faulty Hardware:
What if it is too late?

It's never too late to change. If we have reached adulthood without an adequate supply of coping skills what can we do? We retrain. As adults, having to spend a lot of energy dealing with problems and not being equipped with generic coping strategies to deal with these can stop us living full and productive lives. It stops us meeting one of our deepest psychological needs, that of self-actualisation; a deep-rooted need to be ourselves. We spend so much time feeling inadequate that there is not sufficient mental energy left over to move forward.

What we can do is get creative and fill in the missing bits ourselves. We need to top up the programming.

According to the famous Maslow's hierarchy of needs, after our basic needs are met; of food, warmth, security; and we have a sense of belonging, and feeling valued within our social group; we all have an underlying need to discover who we are so that we can self-actualise. It is the privilege of modern life. It is therefore worth spending the energy to uncover our psychological problems so that we can get on with our personal development. We'd like to be happy or at the very least, live life with some element of contentedness.

In order to be happy, we need to become aware of what things cause us unhappiness.

Anxiety – antithesis to mental health

As a species, we have all learned how to keep anxiety at bay from a very early age, and do it quite naturally. A natural instinct has taught us to do that, which started with our very first cry to tell mummy we were hungry so that we would not starve. Since then we have developed many creative ways of protecting ourselves from harm as best we can, using our instincts and the coping strategies we learned from our parents, friends, schools, yoga classes, and information learned from the media. If anxiety strikes and we haven't got a coping strategy, then our clever biological computer, the brain, has a back-up system and kicks in an ego defence; a natural response the body uses via the brain to protect us and our psyches from harm, as listed in chapter one. These can be less useful and sometimes even harmful in the long run, but will temporarily protect our mental and physical health.

This can be anything from going to see a movie to distract ourselves from our worries, to overeating for comfort, drinking alcohol to forget our troubles, and even using drugs as a way of temporarily switching off the demands of our world.

As well as recognising whether we have a good compliment of coping strategies learned mostly at home and somewhat from our extended community; and understanding that we need to manage our anxiety, we are now ready to review our lives and see if there were defining moments or episodes in our lives which may have impacted on our healthy development.

It is important at this point to emphasize that we are not looking to blame our parents, persons or experiences in our lives for any problems we may have. Parents have likely done their best. It is easy with hindsight to find fault. We are all struggling with knowing what is right and on the whole most people do the very best that they can for their children. That is instinctive. It is their interpretation of what they believe is best that may vary among individuals and is largely to do with how they view their world. It is every parent's privilege to raise their children according to their beliefs and convictions. Nature helps that along by giving parents a deep need to do their best for them.

Psychological Interruptions:
What is a psychological interruption?

Psychological interruptions are those defining moments in our lives when something significant impacts on our familiar routine. Some examples of a psychological interruption can be when someone close to you dies; when a parent suddenly leaves home; when you have an accident and become hurt; when you are suddenly displaced from your home; when you are bullied; when you are humiliated in front of others; and to a lesser extent, when you see a large spider in the bath or you are snarled at by a ferocious dog. Such interruptions to the familiar routine of our day to day lives can cause us huge discomfort and catch us unprepared. We then have to cope with that and hope that we are equipped with strategies that will give us the comfort and strength we need to weather the storm so that we can soon get on with our lives again. If we are fortunate enough to have friends and family to help and support us we will be better off as well.

Unfortunately, we are not all so lucky and many of us will react according to our script and deal as best we can. Let us take the example of a parent suddenly leaving home. In our society it is a common problem these days, but we can imagine a myriad of different scenarios in different homes. We will therefore use one example and incrementally apply similar outcomes to other situations to get a flavour of what can happen.

Let us imagine then that 8 year old Jamie's dad had an almighty row with mum last night and stormed out of the house having taken most of his clothes. Jamie had heard mum shout, "… and I never want to see you again". The thing is, dad was supposed to take Jamie to the football game on Saturday, and Jamie's friend was going to be there with his dad. Jamie laid in bed and felt his heart racing. He felt sick to his stomach and did not know what to do. His world had fallen apart. Everything familiar was now going to be different. He hated his mum for having said that to his dad. He was frightened about the anger. He wanted to cry and be held by mum but how could he when she was responsible. He felt terrified and alone. He could not get to sleep.

For Jamie this is a psychological interruption to the healthy development of his mind. In one day he will have gone from being a boy who lives with a mother and a father to being a boy from a single parent family. If the situation is not handled very carefully Jamie will suffer psychological trauma and a part of him may stop maturing.

What does this separation mean for Jamie? For a start, his primary role model has gone so his gender training has come to an abrupt stop. He may pick up bits and pieces here and there but direct learning of his gender craft will be gone. He may even start to block development as a part of him may say, 'if I can't have dad, I don't want anybody".

The next big loss is father as head of household. Fathers in the family dynamic represent the outside world and Jamie may loose confidence as his connection to the outside world is gone. He has also lost the very important first hand view of how a man and a woman work together as parents and how adults interact with one another.

Next he may begin to struggle with esteem issues as he will no longer feel a part of a solid unit and may feel unsettled about his life. Jamie heard his name come up in the arguments quite often and wondered if it was something about him that made his parents split up. He may feel responsible for the break-up and begin a slow but damaging self-incrimination or self-loathing. His parents may try to protect him from the pain by saying as little as possible to him and leaving chasms of not knowing which may fill with confusion, doubt and misunderstandings.

Damage limitation

That is one example of a psychological interruption and just some of the consequences of its impact on a young mind. If the situation is handled with an element of maturity much damage can be avoided. Mum cannot spare Jamie the pain of loss but both she and her husband can help Jamie understand what is going on and reassure him that it is in no way Jamie's fault. They can assure Jamie that they both still love him and that they will all do their very best to maintain continuity and contact with him. The three can together agree a plan of how they can reduce the pain that the break-up will cause and in so doing the huge upheaval to family life. This way the events that have occurred in Jamie's life will become an experience rather then an unresolved issue which interrupts his psychological development.

More interruptions

Let's have a look at how principal people can hugely affect and influence our lives.

There is no such thing as an intentional psychological interruption. Generally, no one ever intentionally means to cause a person harm and parents do what they feel is best for their children. Sometimes, however, unwitting mistakes can impose life-altering and devastating problems for children.

If, for example a father may have just read some disturbing statistics about boys seducing girls, he may say to his pre-pubescent daughter how dangerous the world is and that 'boys are only ever after one thing'. If each time the subject comes up he alludes to this danger with anger and fear, it may frighten her and she may become terrified of men and sex with men. To the extreme she may become fearful of heterosexual activity and may even choose *homosexuality* as her preferred sexual orientation.

Another disturbing example of misguided parenting affecting a child's development is if a mother catches her four year old masturbating in the bath. If she reacts with horror and tells him that it is a 'sick and wicked thing to do' and she must never catch him doing that again he may be shocked. Some little boys may react with fear and feel uncomfortable ever stimulating themselves this way again. After all, mum is the most important person in his world and she knows what's best.

These people may grow up with *asexual* tendencies, or at the very least, problems with their sexuality.

<u>Cultural Difference</u>
I am a culture baby

We now know that as a species we continually adapt. Charles Darwin knew it. David Attenborough knows it. We know that we constantly adapt to our world and changes in circumstance. We know it is a vital part of our genetic make-up. Not only do we adapt over the long term with skin colour, and body shapes, but we adapt as soon as we exist. We are therefore truly culture babies. From the moment a baby is born he begins adapting to his surroundings. He starts shedding the brain cells that are not required, and building up the ones he needs. He does this simply by reacting to the stimulations of his environment. His body is attuning to his new world. He reacts to hot and cold temperatures and can self-regulate. Although for temperature extremes he depends on his parents to protect him from harm he quickly adapts to the air and climate and gravity.

If a baby born to a mother in the low lands gets chased by enemies high into the mountains then baby's physiology will quickly adapt to the thinner air in his new environment, more so than the adults in the group.

In any environment he neurologically learns to 'get used to' the norms. He internalises sounds and smells as his senses develop accordingly. He learns to feel safe with the continuity of these. He becomes familiar with the faces and sounds of his primary carers and other members of his family as he grows and develops further as part of his world.

A big part of him has already adapted evolutionally as the colour of his skin has, over time, adapted to his climate, and the needs of his society. We know that we have different body shapes, colour, and cultural sensibilities, depending on where we live. In some cold climates both bottom and tops of the eye lids have extra fatty tissue to protect the delicate eye from temperature extremes which looks different from those in warmer climes. Another broad example of this is that in some equatorial cultures people seem to move more slowly and have done so over millennia in order to conserve energy. You know yourself, that when you are in a warm country you find yourself walking more slowly then you might on a Yorkshire high street in October. Northern cultures have learned to keep warm by beetling around more quickly, and thereby generating more heat. They also needed to store food for winter, which meant they had to acquire the skill of long term planning, learning how to gather and store, as the alternative was starvation and death.

My private logic

There are nearly seven billion people on the planet. They are all different. Each individual has his own personal logic, his own way of looking at things. It is their individual way of understanding their world. Our brain knows and understands this. Our heart is often confused by this. We have an intelligent way of looking at things and an emotional way of looking at things. For example, each time we watch a programme on television presented by David Attenborough about the animal world our brain is upgraded with new information and this information adjusts our emotional view of things. If we are really annoyed by caterpillars in our garden and we learn that they have a useful function in the food chain then we may become more tolerant of them and next time not feel so angry when one is munching his way through our cabbages.

Therefore information can change our view of things. Our personal logic is the accumulation of information learned from our social group. Sometime after our fifth year when we really begin to make sense of the information we log these ideas deep into our sensibilities. It is then computed for automatic recall and by association we apply feelings and other senses to the information. Once this information is lodged deep into our minds it feels normal to us. That is how the adaptation process works and makes us similar to the rest of our social group. These feelings are lodged deep into our psyches along with our universal sensibilities, such as a need to love and protect our children. That makes us who we are, all different but all with equal value.

I want to belong

Life is tough for everyone. You may think that the chap driving his new Porsche, or the family in the big house up the road have it easy but everyone struggles with both the logistics of day to day life and dealing with other individuals. We all work hard, constantly, to live our lives well, and protect ourselves from harm. If we have dependents we help and protect them as best we can.

Within our culture we measure ourselves by our peers and create a community to feel a part of. That again is evolutional, as we need to have a sense of value and want to be a valuable member of that group. The reason for that is that a group looks out for one another, and there is strength in numbers.

Most people need an extended community of about two hundred people in their lives; some more, some less, depending on their personality. So when Gavin Jones comes to London from his small village in Wales, he cannot understand why people are not chatting with one another on the underground. He feels unsettled as a result. It may feel cold and uncaring to him. He may not understand that in a large city we cannot possibly become friendly with everyone we see because our psyches would simply blow a fuse. We, therefore, carefully select persons and individuals whom we want in our lives, such as some neighbours, colleagues and friends, and let those in. Gavin Jones needs to understand and respect that.

So, if we have grown up in a small community and move to a large city, this may be confusing for us and may leave a person with a sense of feeling overwhelmed. It may produce anxiety or depression as there could be a sense of losing oneself in the crowd. Alternatively, someone moving from a city to a small community may also feel uncomfortable and miss the anonymity that the city gave him. He may feel watched and judged.

We also measure ourselves against people we admire, or against a group we want to be a part of. In our Western society it can be associated with making lots of money, a common interest in sport or the arts, or those who follow intellectual pursuits. Affluent people can measure themselves against persons in their economic group just like other cultural groups do. Perhaps you admire famous film stars, football players or renowned academics. So if you imagine that "rich or famous people have it made" then you may be wrong, as "the rich and famous" work just as hard to be accepted within their social group. Whether we like to admit it or not, we have a natural yard stick by which we see where we stand by comparison. We look for people similar to ourselves or aspirationally higher to get some notion of how we would like the world to see us and where we fit in. This is often done unconsciously as we go about our business.

Most of us like to associate with someone who has 'importance' so that by association it makes us feel important. The more important we are the less harshly we will be judged by our peers.

His is bigger then mine
Men may measure each other in their pecking order by the size of their houses because it reflects how much money he earns, while women may be competitive by how it looks on the inside as hers is the reflective glory of what skills she was able to offer the relationship. A woman would walk into her neighbour's house and both consciously and unconsciously measure her neighbour's worth by how it looks. There may be no malice involved in this judgement but it is simply done to measure how and where we stand in relation to our peers. "Nice curtains, but I would never put those colours together!"

It is entirely individual and much to do with a person's mental health how much energy and anxiety each and every one of us spends to be accepted by our social group.

I can do that
Recently our lives have been made more interesting by the plethora of DIY programmes on television and there are now many and more creative ways to impress friends and neighbours. With the amount of home, garden and cookery improvement programmes we can use our skills to become more valuable to the group, with a new optimism rather then a competitive criticism. It is a less anxious way of boosting our social confidence. Having some fun with being creative can bind the

entire country together into a small community as we all feel very familiar with iconic gurus like Delia Smith and Jamie Oliver, Alan Titchmarsh and DIY SOS's, Nick Knowles.

With these admired teachers and new more achievable goals, we can all become cleverly more adept at making the most of talents we have. This gives us more attainable and healthy competition amongst our peers within our social group. Having these skills and being able to attribute them to these famous big names gives us bigger value in our social group.

As a fringe benefit, what these programmes do is cross social barriers and unites them so that social differences are not so different. As our economy improves and social classes begin to drift into each other, then boundaries become blurred to non-existent. Social walls come down and everyone is entitled to equal respect. We cling to our peer group in order to belong but our fear, intimidation and anger with other classes dissipates a little more as society matures. We know that sustained fear and anger compromises our health. Anything that reduces fear and anger is helpful and saves ill health.

So, it is important we know and understand who we are. It is even more important that we like and accept ourselves in order for our minds and bodies to be healthy and to thrive. For this reason, we seek contentment and happiness, both for ourselves and for our children. Whether we like it or not, much of what we are is internalised from our parents. We will have adopted their behaviour and the way they interacted with husband, wife and other members of their family as our basic structure for life. We will add or subtract bits we admired or didn't like.

From the moment we are born we will be affected by the way we are treated, how we are handled, how we have behaviour modelled to us, and how our behaviour is managed. If what we learned compliments our innate needs we will thrive. If the way we were treated conflicts with our natural needs then we will have problems, and just as our parents had to deal with the problems they inherited, that will be our legacy.

Chapter THREE
WHAT CAN I DO?

Am I content and happy?

If you feel there is something wrong and you are not content or happy then you need to try to understand why that may be.

We will describe *contentedness* as having your needs met, and *happy* to mean that you are getting on and pursuing what you want from your life. Alternatively, we will then say that the opposite of feeling content and happy might be to feel anxious and unhappy. Depression is helpless unhappiness.

In the 'hierarchy of needs'[6] we are reminded of what we need, for physical and mental health.

1) First we need food, water and warmth, without which we would die.

2) Next we need safety and security.

3) Thirdly, we need a sense of belonging; to be a valued member of our social group.

4) After that, we need a curiosity; a wondering about the world around us. We want to understand its peoples, arts and culture.

5) Lastly, we need a strong enough self-concept, so that we can seek self-fulfilment. We want to understand our selves in relation to the universe. We want self-actualisation.

In order to reach the point of having a good grasp on meeting these needs, we must be trained by our parents and social group so that we don't waste our time feeling inadequate. We need to have internalised sufficient coping strategies and life skills to look after ourselves, and have an ability to creatively solve problems in order to deal with what life throws us. Once we have achieved the creative skills to look after ourselves, we then have time and energy to look after those in the group who are too young, weak, infirm, or elderly. In order for a social group to function it needs this sense of purpose which supporting the larger community gives the individual. Helping those we care about gives a huge sense of purposefulness and produces in our bodies a good balance of health producing chemicals.

As our society became more sophisticated, and we learned to barter with money we were also able to put a little extra money in the pot to help those who cannot help themselves. These taxes then also gave us the means to put people in charge of doing things most of us haven't got time for in our day to day routine so that they help manage the group. They are the politicians. We elect such persons democratically and elect a head of state, and pay these people to make informed decisions on our behalf while we get on with looking after our families and community.

That's the theory. Ideally it should work. The snag is human weakness and if you put someone in charge of your money you need to be able to trust them. It is of course not always the case. We do our best as the group is now so big it needs a lot of man-power to maintain it and it's a constant race for the best jobs. Systems need to be in place to protect the group as best as possible.

Me first

But first you need to look after yourself. You are no good to anyone else if you don't look after yourself first. If you are in an airplane and there is a problem with the cabin air pressure then oxygen masks will appear. It is made clear that before you help dependents you first place the oxygen mask on yourself. You are no good to those who depend on you if you are lying unconscious on the floor.

Often people will feel selfish seeing to their own needs, but the above principal applies. We need a healthy ego. We learn this from our parents. A boy cannot admire his father if his father thinks poorly of himself. A girl will not want to emulate her mother if her mother has no self-respect. We have a responsibility to our children to model useful and mature behaviour to them. Children have a natural sense of what is right and wrong, and that they need to learn maturity. They need from their parents the clues of behaviour within their social group. If the parents or primary carers lack maturity, the children can not learn it. They will feel frustrated, and deep down may resent those who failed them.

Why do I feel so bad?

Now we come to the difficult part. This is why we have psychology, the study of the human mind. It is that most of the very important years during which our brains are programmed are lost to pre-memory. The most important years for programming are the first five years of our lives. This five year period is the time when we learn the vital foundation information, and which is the base of everything we build our futures on. It is the software programming our hardware. It is the information our parents and our world have taught us which we have learned and absorbed. Unfortunately, we have no memory of most of it before the age of four.

In there lies the mystery of behaviour. That is our biggest barrier to uncovering our problems. This is why many of us need help in understanding why we behave as we do. We need trained specialists to help us unlock the secrets of why we feel the way we feel.

What can I do to help myself?

If you are feeling unsettled, unhappy, or even depressed, you will want to have a tool to handle that. First, it is important to understand that generally, these feelings are nothing to be afraid of. These are normal emotions that we feel from time to time just like we feel settled, happy, and excited. And, just like these don't last forever, neither will the negative feelings.

Next, let us check your tool box. What coping strategies have you learned in your life to deal with things? Coping strategies are the tools we learn to use to protect ourselves from harm. These can vary within social groups or families.

To protect ourselves from harm we need boundaries. We have physical boundaries, such as fences to keep toddlers from running into the road; walls to protect our properties; and a good 18 inches of social space between each other when we are speaking to people.

We also have emotional boundaries and learn to protect our private space. We do this with ritualistic social chat such as answering 'fine, thanks', when someone asks how you are even though you have a huge blister on your heel, your cat has just been sick all over your new trousers and you had to cancel a night out with your best friends because your mother-in-law is coming for an unexpected visit.

How we reinforce these boundaries varies from person to person, family to family and culture to culture. Some use ritualistic social niceties. "No dear, I'd rather you didn't sit there as it is my chair and I always sit there." Some people do it with anger, "did you get your driving licence out of a cereal packet?", while yet others use persuasion or even emotional blackmail, "please, darling, I really need all of us to be there or I will have one of my migraines". If those boundaries are threatened you will call on your learned coping strategies to protect yourself from harm. If you meet someone whose coping strategies are different from yours you may have conflict.

What's my strategy?
One example of differing coping strategies is when a young couple marries they spend the first part of their relationship living in euphoric bliss. At some point they may have their first argument. One of the pair shouts at the other. The other says, "whoa, that hurts. Don't do that again." The other may then back down, and apologise and explain about a bad day at work and that they are feeling upset. They talk. If, however, the other did not say "Whoa, etc" and had instead, backed off, the first may shout more and louder because no boundary has been set. The other may back off even further as that person may have

never learned to deal with conflict, and retreat into the kitchen or the garden and busy themselves. The first person is then left with huge frustration and fury because s/he will never find out how far he can go when they loose their temper. They will not know when they are hurting their partner. Eventually, both may begin to resent the other for not being able to help or understand. One uses anger to set his boundaries. The other is passive, and has an expectation that everybody sets passive boundaries. Over time one may feel anger often and the other may feel depressed. They will both soon be angry and depressed, because they both feel helpless.

What if I'm depressed or angry?

If you are *depressed*, it generally means that you have an unresolved frustration. When you are angry or frustrated and it has no where to go, or you don't know how to resolve it, it feels like an unmanageable and futile problem. You feel depressed because of unresolved anger, frustration or fear. You feel helpless.

It is then time to think very hard to try to *identify* what frustration you are sitting on. You need to name the frustration and see if there is anything that can be done to resolve it. You may want to talk to a friend or get some help with this. Depression is often a helpless fear. If you can identify in words what that fear might be you are then in a better position to deal with it.

Next it is important to *look at the consequence* of the fear. For example if you are depressed because of feeling misunderstood by someone then it is important to see what would be the consequence of that. If the consequence is that you might be judged harshly by that person then it means that you rely on that person to see things your way in order for you to function. If that is the case then you are limiting yourself to living your life filtered through someone else's sensibilities. To use a cliché, you have given your power away to that person. You need to regain your personal value so that you have your control back.

If your bowl is empty and you rely on someone else to fill it up then you are reliant on others. If you fill your own bowl then you become self reliant. (see Depression, section 2)

Once you understand why you are depressed you can *do something about it.* One practical way to deal with depression is distraction. Start filling your calendar with activities, particularly fun ones, and get yourself moving with exercise. Start with some very funny films after your first walk. Make someone else your focus so that you get a break from worrying about yourself, and when you feel better you can review how your lifestyle has you locked into a way of life that is making you unhappy. List your options and get to work. Take practical steps to resolve your issues and start ticking your boxes. Then take your rightful place in your social group and say, "Move over world – I'm back!".

Anger, on the other hand is actually fear. Anger is fear of the consequences of losing control. If someone is threatening your life and you can no longer run then your options are few and your defence is 'attack' to survive, or 'regress' to a child-like state and crumble with fear. It is the same with emotional threat. Our bodies react in the same way. It is a perceived threat to our lives. Evolutionally, our bodies react exactly the same way to an actual threat as to a perceived threat; the same to a lion roaring as mother-in-law showing her disapproval.

When someone is angry it is often a reaction to feeling out of control. You may get angry in a car behind a bad driver. You may get angry with your wife or husband, or son or daughter because you have no control over their behaviour. You may get cross with a shopkeeper because he is not stocking what you need. You may get very cross with a neighbour for letting his dog foul on your street. You feel helpless. You can ask yourself, what is the actual threat? For example if your daughter has told you she is going out when you have told her 'no', you feel angry and out of control You then need to ask yourself what is the fear. Is it the discomfort that this may be the beginning of no longer knowing where she is all the time, or is it her welfare that concerns you if you feel she is not old enough to be out and about, or is it something else? You need to understand that it is the consequence of losing control that frightens you and the anger is your tool to try to take control.

Once you understand what your fear is, then you can rationally decide what you want to do about it. If there is something you can do (a letter to the council about dog fouling) then do it. If there is nothing you can do, then cut your losses. Anger will only do you harm.

Anger is the evolutional reaction to danger and our bodies summon up huge reserves to fight or fly. It was never designed to be used as often as we use it, just because we may feel threatened by other people's behaviour. It is huge wear and tear on the body. Anger is the fear of what will happen if your grip is loosened.

Why cry?

You may feel so angry that you will cry. If you cry in private, it is good as it releases a stress hormone and relieves the physical effects of anger. If you cry in front of others it is likely to be a childlike reaction to a frustration. When a person cries in front of others, they are saying, "please take care of me because I can no longer cope".

Because some of us may be lacking in having a good supply of coping strategies learned from our parents, we may struggle when faced with problems we are unfamiliar with. A man may be so fed up with the anger he was exposed to in his family while he was growing up, that he will seek out a passive mate, and then feel frustrated when she does not know how to respond when he is angry, which is his way of dealing with frustration.

Anger in modern society is of course, the province of a toddler and is not the most mature way of dealing with frustration. If, however, it is how your parents modelled coping with frustration, then it is most likely how you will deal with it. This is why it is good to have two parents as there is a good chance you will learn that there is more then one way to resolve things, and choice adds a greater dimension. If you have a richly extended family you have even greater access to learning effective coping strategies.

With a single parent you learn one way of coping and become very fixed in your ways. That is not healthy. With two parents you learn that there is more then one way of doing things, and that gives extra dimension and greater chance for maturity not to mention survival. For their mental health, single parents need to make sure that their children have other principal people in their lives that care for them, which include both sexes.

Anxiety
How do I deal with anxiety?

Anxiety is a very debilitating disorder. It affects most of us in one way or another at some time in our lives. Anxiety is the antithesis to mental health. Anxiety happens if our bodies have been told there is impending danger. It is an evolutional state of readiness for battle. Unfortunately our bodies react the same way to real danger as to perceived danger. Modern life is filled with perceived danger.

Anxiety is your body telling you that your brain has an unresolved issue. This time you may only be at the office living in fear of bullying without sufficient strategies to protect yourself from harm. For example, if you come from a family where people use passive ways of setting boundaries, and you suddenly come into contact with assertive or aggressive persons then you will be at a loss to protect your boundaries. They may 'borrow' your pen and 'forget' to return it. You may continually get targeted to sponsor everybody's charity rides and don't know how to say no, or you are the one always working late doing the donkey work. What's worse, you have a feeling they are all laughing at you behind your back.

Perhaps you are constantly the target of bullying. If this kind of abuse is not dealt with it begins to affect your physical health. If you are at a loss to know what to do to help yourself against the effects of anxiety you have problems Anxiety keeps many people stuck in a way of living which is difficult to change.

A symptom of anxiety is often early waking. In our normal sleep cycle we first have a half hour REM (rapid eye movement) sleep, throughout which our mind processes our thinking, after which we drift into approximately an hour of deep slow-wave sleep when our bodies regenerate and healing happens. We then drift once again into REM sleep. This cycle continues and as we get closer to the morning hours and we become more rested, the slow-wave sleep diminishes and REM sleep increases until finally we are awake, feeling rested and processed.[7]

If we are suffering with anxiety it means that we are in a constant state of readiness for impending danger so that our bodies are in a constant state of alert and never really go into nourishing deep sleep. We become more tired and more anxious and this continues to get worse as the cycle plays havoc with our health.

Sustained anxiety can compromise the immune system and slowly begin to erode our health. Chronic anxiety can double the risk of illness and diseases including headaches, skin conditions, asthma, diabetes, and even heart diseases and cancers. It is therefore in everyone's interest to keep anxiety at bay.

What causes anxiety?

Anxiety is fear. Anxiety is caused by unresolved anger. Unresolved anger is unresolved fear. Like anger, it is fear of the consequence of the unresolved anger. This can be sustained or chronic. This is important. When anxiety takes hold you feel helpless. It can then spiral out of control and at its worst you are reduced to infant status.

For example, when a person is working in an office, his esteem is high as he has been hired to do a job. Therefore someone felt he had value. One day he finds that a colleague may treat him in a way that undermines him. He doesn't have a coping strategy to help himself. This continues. Slowly and insidiously it begins to affect him. He feels tense at work and soon dreads going to work. His metabolism is in a constant state of low-level anxiety. Each time this colleague speaks to him he is in danger of being humiliated in front of his other colleagues. He begins to live in fear of any interaction with this person. He feels misery. He is very angry with this person who is in his estimation spoiling his life. He would like to do anything to make it go away, but he can think of nothing he can do. Any action is deemed futile. He becomes depressed. He becomes withdrawn.

Days and weeks pass, and he feels very unhappy. There is a constant strain on his immune system. He catches colds, and any flu that is going around. He feels a tightening in his chest. His shoulders begin to ache and he regularly sees his doctor. He takes medication which makes him drowsy and he takes time off work. At the office his state of mind is making it difficult to concentrate and his work suffers. His bosses are losing confidence in him. He is not getting the promotions which they hoped he would be qualified for by now.

More time passes and finally he quits his job. He stays home. He feels more and more down. He seldom goes out and being reclusive is becoming a way of life. The less he goes out the more his confidence suffers, and he stops taking care of himself. His depression is now chronic and he becomes nearly fully helpless. He is afraid of dealing with his world.

He has spiralled into infancy. He can no longer take care of himself, and function normally in the wider world. What now? How has this been allowed to happen? All because this man did not have the coping strategy or life skill to stand up to the office bully!

The disturbing thing is that the man may not even have been a bully. Bully boy may just have been a flamboyant character who didn't realise that his behaviour was causing this man such grief.

Many people find themselves losing confidence like this and spiralling down and down into helplessness. You have allowed yourself, in effect to become a helpless infant.

The only way out of this abyss is to push yourself out of your comfort zone and get back into your world. It is not easy but the alternative is to sink into a zone of emotional dysfunction; helpless infancy. It is then time to decide how you want your life to be and to push yourself out there. You are human and therefore have energy and resilience. Only you can figure out what you want and how to get it. Only you have your emotional and physical interest at heart and only you have an obligation to care for you. Once you are an adult, nobody owes you. Your life is your responsibility. That's how it works. Others can support and that is their privilege, but your life is yours.

More anxiety

A practical way to help yourself against the effects of anxiety is to ask yourself what is making you anxious. For example if your bills are mounting up and your rent is due tomorrow and you have no means of finding the cash then you may feel anxious. Your body is reacting because your brain is not listening. Avoiding thinking about your problems will not make the problems go away and they will continue to bubble away in your unconscious, still making your body anxious. Your brain needs to resolve the problem and the anxiety will go away.

You need to: a) Identify the problem. b) Make a list of your options. c) Find a solution. d) Make a mature decision. You can then break the problem down into manageable bits and tackle it one step at the time. With debt problems there are institutions you can go to for help. Once you have dealt with your anxiety effectively, you have learned a coping strategy. You can adapt this new skill to help solve other future problems.

Anxiety is your body somatising unresolved issues. Your body will start to show symptoms of anxiety. It is a warning to the brain that something needs dealing with. Left to its own devices the body will kick in an ego defence to protect itself which could leave you helpless. You may drink more or eat more or find another opiate to drug yourself with which will only temporarily mask the problem. You may go into denial and then start to present with physical problems such as terrible headaches, for example.

If something is causing you anxiety you need to recognise it before it makes you ill, and then develop a coping strategy to deal with it. Failing that you may spiral into helplessness. The problem then falls to those around you to deal with it.

The best way to deal with anxiety is to identify the problem and then decide what needs to be done. You will very likely *need to push yourself out of your comfort zone* to do it, but practice will soon make it easier and you will be back on the road to recovery. Your confidence may even be higher because you feel more in charge of your life. For example if something has made you lose confidence driving on the motorway, then the notion of driving 70 miles to see your mum is going to create anxiety for you. You can take the easy short term solution by avoiding driving but as your confidence erodes more the problem gets worse and anxiety increases. You may need to step out of your comfort zone and like we all know that you need to get straight back on your bike when you fall, you do the drive, *alone*, until your confidence comes back. It will come back and you will feel great.

Addictions, phobias, fetishes and other attachments
So we cope as best we can with the tools we have. If as children we felt anxious and needed comfort we relied on our parents to provide that. They would then help us and show us what to do. If they did not, then ego defences kicked in which is our immature brain needing to protect us from stress. We then learned to either run from whatever caused us fear or run to

something for comfort. This is the time when phobias (running away for comfort) or fetishes (running to something for comfort) can manifest. If these are neurologically hardwired before the brain reaches adulthood they become part of a person's shaping and will feel normal.

Attachment
In order to understand addiction and many anxieties, we need to understand the concept of attachment.

<u>healthy attachment</u>
When a child is born he is in a symbiotic relationship with his mother. When she places him in a cot for longer then he is comfortable with, he experiences separation anxiety. He cries tearless cries to let her know he is feeling insecure. She picks him up and he re-attaches to her, and feels comfort. One day she chooses to ignore his cries. Baby frantically seeks maternal comfort and finds a soft surface or cloth and re-attaches himself to it. He sleeps. When he wakes he cries for the familiar comfort of his mother and finds the cloth which smells of him and her and he feels familiar comfort and he sleeps. Baby has re-attached himself for comfort to an inanimate object. He is partially detached from his mother to start the process of independence. The next morning she is reliably there to help him with his day.

<u>healthy detachment</u>
As he grows up he trusts that she is close by for security and comfort. He grows and he thrives. In small stages, and with encouragement she helps him separate until, around the age of 16 he is able to stand alone.

unhealthy detachment

If a child feels anxiety associated with his maternal attachment, that is, if he feels insecure in his development he may detach from her. If, for example, she disapproves of his behaviour in a way that causes him confusion and pain, and he feels he can not get her approval, he will eventually detach himself from her to reduce anxiety and attach to other people or objects in order to seek comfort and fulfil innate needs.

If mother disapproves of him in such a way that he feels valueless he may seek comfort elsewhere, and in desperation may turn to unhealthy attachments in order to help block out uncomfortable feelings. (A disturbing primary care environment may also create anxiety).

unhealthy re-attachment

When a child is disillusioned with his maternal attachment, or he feels unsafe in his environment, he reattaches to something inanimate. The greater the disillusionment, the greater the object he will re-attach to, and the greater will be his detachment from his primary carer. The problem with re-attachment to an inanimate object is that it cannot encourage independence. Therefore once a person is attached to an object, he may be attached for life, as there is no encouragement to become independent of it. Hopefully he will attach to something useful such as work, sport, acting, travelling, etc.

When a person re-attaches to an object that is addictive, such as food, alcohol, drugs, fetishes, etc. then not only will he not become independent of it, but he will be dependant (addicted) to it. An addiction is when the body, for adaptation purposes, integrates a chemical into its needs system.

For normal development, and with our learned life skills, most of us will healthily detach and re-attach to socially acceptable things such as work, sport and even our own new family unit and other life enhancing activities.

A General View of Coping strategies/Life skills

We learn our life skills from our parents and social group. When there is an absence of a life skill our automatic response will kick in to protect us from harm and anxiety. That's not always a good thing. It is important to have a good repertoire of coping strategies to help you cope with your life. We know that it is impossible to know how to deal with all situations, and we all flounder at one time or another. This is when your support system comes in handy. It is lovely to have a family member or a friend who occasionally reminds you that you have value. "Darling, what would we do without you?" Unfortunately, we British are not very good at reinforcing good behaviour or rewarding good efforts. It is therefore not always easy to judge our own value, and it would not take much to chip away at what we do have. Perhaps that is why the pint of bitter or glass of wine is such a popular friend for many of us.

Self-confidence
I am who I am

From the moment we wake up in the morning until we close our eyes to go to sleep at night our unconscious effort is working hard to maintain or improve our social status and avoid humiliation. We therefore do what is familiar and safe and get on with it. If we have suffered embarrassment or we are feeling unpopular we may find ourselves perilously slipping off life's conveyor belt.

If for one reason or another then you are finding it difficult to be in your group, then it may be time to do something, to help your self to feel better. It's time to see what it is you want? This is your one and only life. How do you want to live it? A quote often attributed to Nelson Mandela, Marianne Williamson famously reminds us, "Our deepest fear is not that we are inadequate. Our deepest fear is that we are powerful beyond measure. It is our light, not our darkness, that most frightens us. Your playing small does not serve the world. There is nothing enlightened about shrinking so that other people won't feel insecure around you. We are all meant to shine as children do".[8]

You need a sense of feeling value within your community and a sense of wanting your community to reflect your values. You need a sense of familial pride, community pride, and national pride. Cheesy as it may sound, deep down you know it is in your interest to live in an atmosphere of harmony and co-operation with others around you who are like you and have a loyalty towards each other so that you can function as a group. That's evolutional. As a species we are designed to co-operate in a social group as there is strength in numbers for protection. Alone we are vulnerable. Schools, village and community life mimic those conditions and make us feel a part of a co-operative; something which is fundamentally healthy. Those that live in the city will create their own small community by having favourite shops and a group of friends.

So whether you are large or small, pink or brown, optimist or pessimist, brave or weak, extrovert or introvert or anywhere on the spectrum of any of these or more, you have a life that needs living. If it looks easy for others and hard for you it may be just your perception and what you keep reinforcing your brain to believe.

What everyone admires is someone who can look after themselves so that others can get on with their own lives. That's why we all love winners and try to shut out losers. That may be evolutional. However, evolution has its own agenda. A mature society makes space for everyone and if you are a person then you have a right to your share of space. You might as well enjoy the ride.

Chapter FOUR
PARTNERSHIPS – What happens when they break?

The difference between your relationship with your partner and your relationship with everybody else is sex. It is what sets you as a couple apart from other relationships and makes it personal, private and special.

Most of us dream of one day meeting a partner and together set up house, share a life, and have a family. We hope that we will love that person and that they will love us back. We see evidence around us that many marriages struggle but that does not deter us and we feel sure that for us it will be the right thing.

Marriage or any ceremony to mark the union of a couple is the most natural thing in the world. Even if weddings became unpopular it would continue to reinvent itself because we are a mating animal and when two people fall in love and want to be together, they need to tell their world.

It is an announcement to your community that you have chosen a life partner with whom you want to set up home and start a family. Evolutionally it is a normal and progressive event. This announcement needs to be celebrated. Every social group has its own ritualistic way of doing this. It is a wonderful and important time for any couple and its community.

Our new couple will soon adjust to their new world which will be a combination of his perspective of how a couple ought to live together and how she feels their lives should work as a couple with the possibility of starting a family in the future. Depending on how different their backgrounds are or how they each view marriage they will need to make some compromises until they settle into a workable arrangement. There are some more evolutional genetic triggers at work here as being a deeply intimate sexual couple induces a euphoric bliss which will smooth the way temporarily until a routine is established. We call this love. Love can sustain quite a lot of choppy waters until the couple learns to paddle the boat themselves and this state of excitement can last for anything up to a couple of years. Very often by then a couple may have conceived their first child and on the whole, with two maturing adults the hope and promise of a good future keeps them ticking over.

It is very exciting for each member of this new family to have a special role and makes them feel very grown-up, as they have been in training for their roles most of their lives. With a healthy couple they will soon take up their gender specific roles and because he has a deep conviction that his role is to be the guardian and breadwinner, and she the bearer and carer of children they easily slip into their roles as parents.

However latterly we are beginning to question gender specific roles and our society is beginning to break away from tradition and redefine the rules. So let us see why a conventional male may feel he needs to be the breadwinner of the household. It's quite simple. From the moment he sniffed that he was a male, which is around the age of two he started to direct his own gender training. If he had a conventional home life he would have soon got the message that daddies go out to work every day and earn the money to pay the mortgage while mummies stay in and get pregnant and feed babies. Therefore it is quite a natural result of early training. With plenty of reinforcement his brain would have neurologically shaped itself with this belief. If his home environment had been different; if a pack of wolves raised him, or children, or a cage in a laboratory, or two males or two females, or any deviancy from the norm then his neurological development would have adjusted accordingly and the hard-wiring would be different. He would then view the world differently. However, because it takes a man and a woman to make a baby, the general environment is the conventional one.

Genetically men are bigger and stronger then women and in the old days it made sense that mothers fed the babies and daddies protected (and paid for) the cave. Little children studied their gender from toddler days and hardwired the information into their sensibilities and it became for them a 'deep seated need' to be a good mummy or daddy, and on the whole most of us are up for that. Anything that catches the imagination of the mind by desire or default gets programmed into the biological computer at an early age and becomes a 'deep seated need'. This can include a desire to be a brain surgeon or an astronaut or a just a useful member of your community. Unfortunately, it can also include antisocial desires such as fetishes and other psychopathologies.

Because society is becoming more flexible and because different cultural ways are being tolerated within our social groups it has become clear that we are human products of our environment.

The human element is that men are still bigger and stronger then women and that women carry and breastfeed babies so that part will still need to be accepted for the time being. The environment shapes us. Different personalities make the shaping unique.

However, on the whole the conventional way of life is still consuming most of us and the idea of coupling and family making is still a desirable and exciting option for youngsters coming from conventional backgrounds. Generally they have accepted and embrace their roles and know there is much to be gained from setting up family life. After childhood, home life becomes a little harder and we soon outgrow our family situations. We are then ready to leave the nest. We have also learned that learning a craft to make money makes our lives easier so we take a bit or a lot of time out to do that before or during the time we settle into our own new homes. A strong desire to have our own children then looms and although most of us are still unsure whether that need is evolutional or part of our training, we know that having children gives us a great sense of purpose and becomes a focus for most of us. There is in all of us a very strong evolutional need to nurture and protect that child which healthy people all do unquestioningly and so the cycle continues.

Now comes the tricky bit. Although we generally feel a great loyalty to our offspring, we now often struggle with the relationship itself, and although many marriages still survive and come to happy conclusions, there are now also many relationships in trouble and couples endure deep unhappiness in either staying or leaving the partnership.

What's gone wrong?

For mental health, we need to be a valuable member of our social group. For a relationship to work, we need to feel value within the relationship. If for any reason we do not feel value, whether it is self-imposed or partner imposed, we are in trouble. When we lose our value in the eyes of our partner we have a problem. When we no longer respect our partner we have a problem. If we begin to take our partner for granted we have a problem.

Let's start with what might be considered a traditional young British couple. Colin and Jen met at the local pub on 'pub quiz' night and found they both knew a lot of obscure information which impressed either one about the other. They had such a laugh that evening they wanted to see what else they had in common. With an unconscious desire to meet a complimentary partner, they set about getting to know each other better. As luck would have it all the bits fitted well together. He was 25 years old and she was 23. He had finished college and was working for his dad temporarily as a plumber and she had just got her first job as a p.a. for a small but growing company in town. They enjoyed each others company and soon fell in love and set up house together. They had 3 children and worked hard, and lived to a ripe old age, paying their taxes and supporting their children and grandchildren as best as they could.

This scenario is nice to read because there is no tension in hearing about it as the couple were able to look after themselves, and contributed their bit to society as they managed their lives well.

Because modern society has embraced many different cultures, the rules for normality have changed. For mental health we also need to have some control over our environment in order to feel safe. As children we learn the rules of our society and feel safe within those boundaries, but the boundaries are not so clear anymore as multi-culturalism, television and change in our social world give us new and flexible options. As we grow up we ask our parents to help us make sense of it all, and get their interpretations of how they see it to help us decide how we want to see it. A man and a woman can have learned many different ways of seeing things and it becomes more difficult to find a partner with similar values. If different view points within a partnership threaten the comfort zone of either partner they will become unsettled and react defensively. When a person becomes defensive it is because they are no longer in control of their lives and this loss of control makes them very uneasy.

Things might have been different for Colin and Jen. If somewhere within the relationship Jen had mentioned that she had travelled all over the world with dad because of his job and she wanted to live abroad at some point, a little alarm bell may have sounded in Colin's head but he may have ignored it. When later in the marriage she might have pushed for them to move to Croatia it might have made old home loving Colin very uncomfortable and may have begun a down turn in their life. Alternatively, perhaps Colin may have wanted to go back to Uni and use all the family funds to retrain as his child hood ambition was to be a vet and Jen couldn't settle until she had her own home in a good part of town. There would be a conflict of interest of how money would be spent and either the stronger of the two would win or the relationship might crumble.

Generally when a couple gets together they both know compromises have to be made. The payoff of getting 'needs' met generally compensates. If, however, the balance is wrong and there isn't sufficient pay-off then an unsettledness moves in. A growing resentment may build until it becomes unbearable and one of the couple wants out. Sometimes with help they are able to renegotiate the terms and their life as a couple can continue. Other times they can't.

Alarm bells ringing

Problem solving is a life skill that mature parents teach their children. It is a useful skill to take into a relationship. We learn our coping strategies from our parents and from our social group and if we haven't got a coping strategy to deal with a problem, we now know that an ego defence kicks in. That's generally bad news.

Coping strategies are not all good news either. For example spitting in the boss's coffee when he is not looking because he has just told you that you can't have a raise is not a mature way to handle the situation. Neither is shouting at your child because you have just stepped in a puddle; or the one we all worry about, complaining in a restaurant and having the chef take it out on us by doing something undesirable to our meal.

Mature parents teach their children to share their toys or to take turns, and generally teach lessons of co-operation so that the individual learns that the world works better if all members of the group are content. As a child, an id-driven egocentricity makes you want all the toys and all the sweets but as you mature you come to realise that it is not likely you will be left alone in a corner with all the world's toys and all the world's chocolates and that it will not buy you happiness. We learn that we are happier playing together, sharing our goodies and taking it in turns to play with a coveted toy which seems fairer then not getting to play with it at all. These life skills need to be learned and make us mature enough to operate in a large group and eventually to know how to live with a partner. With maturity we soon start to understand our boundaries within the partnership and learn how to negotiate fairly.

What happens if my rules are different?

If, however your partner has not learned the same rules and negotiation tactics as you then you can have problems. If, for example the first time Jen wanted her way and shouted at Colin, and Colin has no experience in dealing with angry people then they have a problem. If Jen learned in her family that if you really want something you have to shout and have a tantrum and Colin's parents never raised their voices then Colin won't know what to do. He may just go quiet and hope the noise stops soon. He may learn to fear her tantrums and give in to her demands. She will soon have too much power in the relationship and resentments will start to grow. She needs Colin to say, "stop shouting like that, it is undignified and immature. I will talk to you only if you speak to me in a reasonable manner". Then they can move forwards. That will be difficult for Colin as he has no experience in being firm. Equally, Jen could become aware that her way is not working with Colin and that perhaps her life strategy for negotiating leaves a lot to be desired.

Learning new, healthier rules

So, a mature heart fills in the bits the brain has not learned. Learning better life strategies than the ones we learned at home means re-learning with your adult brain. It is not easy and just like a second language it is learned with a different part of the brain. The younger you retrain, the sooner you can incorporate it into your sensibilities. If you have to relearn as an adult, it will be more difficult and you may always have 'an accent'. Learning a new language after the age of twelve often retains an audible accent.

So when you became aware that some of your behaviours may be somewhat anti-social, and yet they feel perfectly natural to you, it may be because it is what you learned when you were young. It may have been a behaviour you adopted in order to avoid anxiety and to feel comfort. That became lodged into your sensibilities (neurologically programmed) and feels normal to you. You then need to decide for yourself whether you want to continue behaving like this. If you are ready to change then with practice and reinforcement you can actively alter it to a behaviour you feel happier with. It will then lodge into your automatic pilot and become a learned behaviour just like driving, cycling or playing the violin.

A brain is a very sophisticated computer, but even the best computers need programming and so does your psyche. You know yourself if you hear often enough that you are boring or stupid or lazy, you eventually begin to believe it. It means that if you play a different recording such as 'I'm good with computers', 'I love working with children', or 'I really must try those new recipes because I want to excel at cooking' these will also find a niche.

It is therefore a good idea to teach life skills in primary schools and hone them at secondary school level. Teaching basic psychology early in secondary schools which includes the benefits of positive reinforcement and that action invokes reaction it would teach children collectively how to behave more sociably and give them a better idea how to behave maturely.

What if I'm unhappy?

This is your one and only life. How do you want to live it? If your mind is immediately drifting off to faraway places in the sun, then go with the fantasy. When you have seen exactly where you would like to be then have another think and see how realistic that is. If you can make it happen and that is the life for you then go for it. If not, then after you have fully relaxed in the fantasy, then think maturely about what your options are and what it would take to get there. Then before you go any further, think hard about what you have if you got there. Here is an exercise borrowed from Dr. Phil[9] in America.

What do you want? I want a black Porsche.

What would it give you if you had that? My friends would think I was cool.

So what you really want is your friends to think you are cool.

So when you have explored what it is you want and what would make you happy, consider hard what you would have if you had what you want. Would it bring you approval or attention? Are you feeling inadequate and need external props to define you. Or is it a personal reward for your own hard work. Is it making a dream come true or a fantasy fulfilled.

Would having what you want make you feel useful or proud? Would it bring a hum to your tune; put a skip in your step? Would you feel proud to go to the next family reunion? Would you feel you had real purpose? Would you feel good?

Of course, that is a fantasy you can explore if you are free and unattached. Life is not always that simple. Most of us have commitments and obligations and those who depend on us. But it is still an exercise worth doing, quite simply to establish what would 'rock your boat' if you had your way.

My life would be just perfect if only my partner would change!

Now back to the real world. If you are in a relationship and you are unhappy it is time to see why that is. As long as there are no children involved it is not that difficult to do something about it. Have you got an idea what is making you unhappy? Are you blaming your partner or are you blaming yourself? Is there a clash of personality and perhaps you do not respect each other's values. Are you feeling undermined? Are you undermining your partner and wish s/he could stand up to you? Do you want your partner to manage you, or do you feel you need to manage your partner? Is everything pretty good 'if only ...'? Do you feel locked into a relationship and you don't know how to get out? Are you afraid of getting out and being lonely? Do you feel trapped?

Sometimes we blame our partners for not being who we want them to be. Are you punishing your partner for not being someone in your expectation? Perhaps you feel you are not meeting your partner's expectations? Do you feel you are being punished for being you instead of being someone who is different?

Spiralling into infancy

Change is unsettling. But if you are unhappy, you can either stay that way or you can do something about it. As an adult, the choice is yours. If you are staying because you are afraid, then you can do something about that by getting outside support. When you are afraid to change your situation it may be because you are frightened of the consequence of that change. This can lead to depression.

The more you avoid looking after yourself the more you regress into a childlike state and the more you lose your confidence as a mature adult who can manage his or her own life. When you feel you are falling apart and say "I can't do this anymore", you are saying to those around you, "I am helpless – you make decisions for me". You then risk spiralling into helplessness and letting others take care of you. You are then dependent.

Change is unsettling but the pay-off may be worth it. For example if you are staying because you don't want to hurt your partner's feelings, ask yourself if pity is the right reason for staying in an unhappy relationship. If you worry that your partner may be angry with you then you have worked out that your partner uses anger as a strategy to control you. If you are worried that you may lose all the money you have invested in the partnership, then a quick visit to a solicitor can soon reassure you that you have rights and protection there. Sometimes you simply have to cut your losses.

When you have been in an intimate relationship with someone and you are now unhappy it may feel wrong to walk away. Nature intends it to be that way as we are a mating animal and once you have set up home with someone and have been deeply intimate with each other you are essentially knitted together for the purpose of starting a family. In our modern society with a world population of nearly seven billion it is no longer a major issue and in a few million years people may not feel that way anymore. But for now it is difficult to walk away from someone you have bonded with. The point is you know from life's experiences that it is possible to find someone else who may be more compatible so that you can have another chance at being happy and to live more respectfully.

Separating is hard and there is no way to avoid pain. There will be loss and loss must be grieved. No one can take that away from you. It is part of the privilege of being human. Emotions need to be endured.

No cheating

The wrong way to separate is the cowardly way to do it. If you are unhappy then you need to let the people involved know. Spitting in the boss' coffee is cowardly and immature. You are an adult. It is only fair to treat others in a way you would like to be treated. If you are philandering then that is unfair. Your partner cannot fight an invisible enemy. If an unspoken contract is sexual loyalty then playing away from home is unfair particularly if you have the opportunity and your partner doesn't. It is deeply humiliating for anyone to find out they have been betrayed in this way.

Just like a child can cope with parents separating if it is handled properly, relationships can cope with separation if handled maturely. If you are id-driven you will just please yourself but if you are mature and you are ego-driven you will consider the needs of the principal people involved including your own, quite simply because if the shoe was on the other foot you would want to be treated that way.

My partner is having an affair

Why would anyone want to risk losing their home life and hurting the principal people in their lives by having an extra marital affair? There may be many reasons. One reason may be precisely that it is a risk and therefore a double pay-off; an internalised permit to play away, and the thrill of the risk. Another reason might be unhappiness with your current marital situation. But it is like spitting in the boss' coffee; a bit underhanded and not very mature. Perhaps they may want to hurt their partner in the hope that they will end the marriage as they are not strong enough to end it themselves. There could be many reasons why partners stray as everyone has their own agenda with their self interest as heart. For most of us, however, the self-interest includes the happiness of those we love and the larger community which serves us.

Affairs are risky things. If one of the couple is having an affair then they are jeopardising the happiness of their family life and risking disrupting the lives of all members of that family. Why would someone do that? What is the payoff?

Jen and Colin have been married for some years now and have 2 children, Josh and Jenny. Colin has moved up the corporate ladder and is now CEO. He feels very important and at the city conference he is paid much attention by his associates and colleagues. He likes the attention. When he goes home his wife seems more interested in researching their new washing machine then how his day went, and chats to him about the characters of her favourite soap opera. She has put on a lot of weight recently and he wonders what it would do for his image if he brought her to the Christmas office party. He is beginning to feel that he is entitled to be in the company of more attractive and dynamic people like himself and feels his life at home does not quite define him the way it ought to. He tells himself that his wife seems unaware of his feelings and does not seem to understand him anymore.

As the job grows he spends more of his energy keeping the strands of his work life in hand. At home it becomes difficult to put them down and he needs a good shot of scotch to relax.

Colin spends more time at the office and now with his colleagues, who are fast replacing his family for the place where he wants to spend his time. His PA is attentive and sees to his every need. She is interested in his work and can discuss his concerns with him in a helpful way. He feels increasingly close to her. When the last recent contract was closed they went for a celebratory drink and felt very close. They sealed that closeness at the conference hotel. Colin felt confused as he feels he loves his wife and children, yet somehow his new relationship does not feel wrong. Colin has split his loyalties. Colin feels entitled to both. Colin has a problem.

Jen and Colin have drifted into separate worlds. Jen is wholly immersed in her world of raising children and keeping a home which she shares with Colin. She feels value in that world. She knows Colin is busy and therefore takes on the management of the home.

Colin has two distinctly separate worlds. He has value in both but feels greater value in his work world. At home he is not the manager and at work he is that plus some. At work he is powerful. His subordinates can't do enough for him. He works hard and begins to wonder what should be his reward for all that hard work. The media and advertising hype make it quite clear, subliminally and otherwise that the ultimate reward is sex. Colin feels a sense of entitlement and rewards himself.

What about me?

Sometimes a woman can feel very insecure because her husband has an important job and she feels threatened by his other life. It makes sense. He knows all about her world as he is immersed in it every time he is home, however, she knows little about his world. If he works late at night preparing for 'the office' she may see his work as a mistress; a love and loyalty he has for it which does not include her. She will need extra reassurance that he loves her and that the work is a means to an end. Sometimes words alone are not enough and she will need him to understand her insecurity and show evidence that his work does not threaten their relationship.

Spot the danger zones

So why do some people have affairs and others don't. There are as many reasons as there are people in the world to have them. Some may include the following:

- Sometimes it is to do with the thrill of risk-taking.

- Sometimes it is boredom.

- Sometimes sex is seen as a reward for doing a good job and little to do with the intimate act.

- Sometimes a man or a woman may feel inadequate with a partner who may undermine them and feel better with someone else, but not strong enough to leave the relationship.

- Sometimes a man or a woman may have a fantasy about having sex with someone else and cannot rest until it has been explored.

- Sometimes someone who is very id-driven may have a great sense of entitlement and simply feels he deserves to have sex with more women and is not worried about the consequences of the affair.

- Sometimes a person may be very angry with their partner and uses an affair as a way to hurt them.

- Sometimes a person may be very angry with their partner and uses an affair as a way of seeking comfort.

- Sometimes, the threat of an affair can be very controlling and a powerful ploy.

- Sometimes sex with someone else feels less emotional than with a partner.

It is difficult to come to terms with the pain of infidelity within a relationship. Relationship experts however find that many marriages do survive it. It is as perennial as the storms at sea. Internalised coping strategies or ego defences allow the affair and then consequences follow; all part of the rich tapestry of life. How we deal with these is what is important. There will be various options, and the ones which keep pain and anxiety at bay will be the preferred one.

Everything would be just great, if only ………..

When you have a problem it becomes a focus. For example if everything is ticking along nicely and you manage to work out problems and have a healthy respect for the different members of the family then all is well. If all is well except money becomes a problem then that will become a big focus in your life. If you find you are often arguing about money then money becomes an unhealthy focus in the relationship, and the source of many arguments.

So it is with any big problem. If you have problems with sex then it becomes an unhealthy major focus in your lives. If you find you have issues about the way you want to teach or influence your children then that will be a problem in the relationship.

It is impossible for two people to agree on everything and healthy debate and accepting each others difference of opinion is good. It is good for children to see parents debating and seeing them resolving issues. In fact it is much healthier then having a single parent and internalising all their logic with the added danger of becoming very fixed in your thinking. Debate in the household precipitates creative thinking and needing to find workable solutions.

All families fight at one time or another. That's normal too. It is how the fights are resolved that determines maturity and growth.

If there is a problem in a relationship that is not resolved it can rumble, create misery and get in the way of healthy interaction.

What about the children?

When you are unhappy in a relationship and there are children to consider you have a very big problem. We have a deep and great need to protect our children from harm and rightfully so. Their young minds are on a mission to grow up, achieve and learn, and maintain mental health and when the family unit is threatened there is danger. Their personal development is threatened as they will feel great anxiety which is harmful and debilitating. As parents we know that and go to great lengths to prevent any harm coming to them. Most mature parents will go through fire and hell for their children and their personal happiness easily comes as a last priority. The question is, at what point do they realise that even their personal sacrifice is not enough?

The good news is that children can handle parent separation if it is handled properly. Children need to be protected from the pain their parents are experiencing but of course that is not always possible. If children are exposed to the drama of their parents' break up then they will feel very frightened. This will manifest in lots of different types of behaviour changes and 'acting out' because they haven't got the skills or sophisticated mental faculties to deal with this. Ego defences will kick in. The kindest thing to do is to protect them as much as you can from your pain, and when the inevitable has to happen, to reassure them that

a)   it is not their fault

b)   that mummy and daddy still love them

c)   keep them updated on any major changes that will involve them, and let them tell you how they feel about that

d)   do your talking during the day, and keep evenings as routine and secure as you can

e)   listen to them but do not let them start to make decisions about the new regime. They need to know that mum and dad may be splitting up but that they are all still safe within the new boundaries.

It is impossible to protect them from the pain they will have to endure but under the right conditions these can become experiences that help shape them rather then traumatic events that will harm them.

Step-parents

Step-parenting is a tricky business. In a relationship with a man or woman who is not the biological parent of your children there is often a frustration which is difficult to recognise. As a couple you may be very fond of one another, and the children have accepted the new person in the home, however, when there is conflict problems can happen. Very often a mother will feel divided loyalties between both her children and her new partner. Depending on the ages of her children she will feel the need to love and support her children first and foremost. She then feels guilty not to support first her partner. He may be putting her in a position where she feels she has to choose between them.

What is happening here is that her first loyalty is to her children. Her new partner's first loyalty is to her. She knows her children still need her but from her partner's perspective the children are placing heavy demands on the woman he loves. Because they are not biologically his, he does not have an intrinsic loyalty to them. To him it may look like they are asking too much from their mother. He may feel a great need to love and protect her however a child's job is to be the perfect parasite until he has learned from her to fend for himself. It is difficult for a step dad to accept and understand that. There is a conflict of interest. There is inevitable strife.

A Healthy relationship

We strive to be healthy adults. We want to be in a healthy relationship. A healthy relationship is one where two people accept each other as individuals and respect each other. Neither depends on the other to define them. They each have a strong self-concept and know that they could stand alone if they had to but choose to be together.

However, they take pride in their union. A healthy couple respect each other and value their home and the family aspect of that home. It gives them great comfort to be a unit and both partners understand the risk of losing everything if they strayed out of their boundaries; the written and unwritten rules they set when they became man and wife.

They know it is not always easy and at times either of their loyalties can be tested when the overwhelming responsibilities of the partnership or parenting push them to their limits. They know they have a lot together, and they know they have a lot to lose. They are aware of each others imperfections and can tolerate these as they are aware of their own shortcomings. They both understand that as long as there is sufficient pay-off for effort spent that all is well with the world. They also know that when all is not well they have each other to hold tight to in order to weather the inevitable storms.

Life is hard but predictable and has many compensations.

Chapter Five
HEALTHY CHILDREN BECOME HEALTHY ADULTS

We are egoistic enough to believe we have a lot of control over our lives, but, let's face it, we are merely custodians of ourselves and for a limited time, of our children. Once our child is conceived much is out of our hands. As it develops, a series of genetic triggers brings our offspring to birth and infancy, puberty, menopause and eventually death. We can only marvel at this phenomenal sequence of events. A beguiling infant develops into a beautiful and marvellous child. Then, a genetic trigger decides, oops, it is time to make this person into a sexual being and suddenly changes begin to alter and mature the body. This pro-creative phase lasts until approximately age 50 and another trigger decides that time is up and a degenerative process begins. Some hormones are withdrawn and nature kindly begins its slow and gentle process of withering until our bodies are finished. We generally accept this without question.

What we do have some control over is how we manage our lives and treat our children. We have some say in how we prepare them for adulthood. Most of us will do this using the values we grew up with and mimic the methods used by our parents, adding and subtracting bits we wished were there and bits we didn't like. Hopefully, we include and blend these ideas with those of our partners. Add to that some modern ideas and we feel we have a formula for doing a good job. The ultimate hope is that we can raise happy, responsible children who will be able to eventually care for themselves when we are no longer able.

Of course, nothing is so straightforward and we know that in that notion lie some snags. We can no longer fully rely on what feels natural to us. Psychologists know that early years programming, once adopted and put into our automatic pilot will then forever feel normal to us. They know that sometimes such programming is wrong and can lead us astray. This may vary from harmless misconceptions, such as 'walking in the rain makes your hair grow faster', or 'eating your bread crusts makes you a better whistler', to more harmful ideas such as 'smacking a child is good discipline'. We know fetishes and phobias, anxieties and addictions can be the result of poor or harmful early programming.

It simply means that occasionally it is prudent to check to see that you have got it right. It is mature to be aware that even though something feels normal that it is not necessarily so, and we all have misconceptions and fallibilities.

My child is better then your child

It is a delicate balance and to get it right, parents need a good portion of maturity. We all want the best for our children, but at what cost? Playgroup sports day and we are encouraging little Simon to run as fast as he can. Hooray, he wins and you show your deep pride and approval. He feels huge value. He also has an experience of what it feels like to be a winner. Briefly, that is excellent programming for his repertoire.

His friend Timmy was last. He is devastated. Mum gives Timmy a hug and dad assures him he is still loved and cared about.

All is well in the social group. For mental health, Simon now has to hope that he does not have to win all the time in order to have value and Timmy has to hope that, even if he never wins a race, that he will be good at other things to give him social value. These thoughts, of course, are unconscious, however real and will sow seeds in their mental development.

Had either or both of Timmy's parents shown disappointment, Timmy may have started on a long and painful road with self worth issues and gender issues.

When Simon sees Timmy he gives him a pat on back and shows him his medal. Timmy gets to hold it and both boys go and play. Simon and Timmy are aware that their value is not dependent on winning or losing races.

A Summary:
A brief summary of what a parent can do for their child to give her or him the best chance of becoming a mentally healthy adult.

A child needs:
1) protection from harm
2) to learn coping strategies
3) to learn the rules of his social group
4) to feel he belongs
5) to feel he has value
6) unconditional acceptance
7) to learn the life skills for independence

Protection from harm – this includes
a)   food and warmth, without which he will die
b)   physical boundaries, including such things as a fence to stop him from running into the road, dangerous things put out of reach, etc.
c)   curfews, as a child needs to feel safe in the knowledge that parents are setting his limits which are in his best interest.
d)   protection from predators – if a child is being abused physically or sexually he should be educated and informed that such things are wrong, and feel safe in the knowledge that when he tells parents or a responsible adult that they will believe and help him.
e)   protection from over-eating – if your child is gaining inappropriate weight then it is the responsibility of the parent to manage that. Children rely on their parents to provide food for them, and it is your job to provide, as best you can, what they need for healthy development.
f)   protection from harmful substances – Drinking alcohol or using opiates in front of your children gives him instant

permission to do the same. All your behaviour models to them behaviour they will consider copying. It is part of your remit to educate at age-appropriate times about the dangers of harmful substances. It is also your responsibility to protect them from these until they are old enough to make such decisions for themselves. If you cannot always be there to police it, then you can do your best to inform them of the dangers so that they are suitably equipped to help protect themselves.

To learn coping strategies

This may seem obvious, but coping strategies are learned. When a child falls and hurts himself he may panic and cry. His mum will come running, help him up and soothe his pain. She may rub the wound, show him how and why it happened and suggest to him he watches more carefully for hazards when he is running. With this information logged, the next time he falls, there will be less panic until such incidents root into his psyche. He will see that sometimes people have accidents and that these can be survived. He will internalise the skill of soothing, learn to self soothe when mum is not there, and eventually be able to soothe others. He has a useful coping strategy in his repertoire.

Other such coping strategies can include learning to deal with failing a test, loosing a race, having a favourite toy broken, loosing a valued object, being bullied, and so on.

To learn the rules of his social group

This was easy in tribal days. Boys learned hunting and gathering skills from the men and girls learned housekeeping and cooking skills from the women. Rituals and group behaviour was straightforward and easily reinforced. As the world population swells and boundaries become less defined, we need to be alert and skilled to provide for our children the demands of our evolutional instincts. For many of us, much confusion is thrown into the mix and we rely heavily on our social group to guide us.

As we grow more multi-cultural we try to embrace different ideas and this is helped along with popular television programmes and easily accessible media information. We are therefore more able to imprint onto our children a more mature social conscientiousness which includes social empathy, sharing, tolerance, and acceptance.

Children need to learn from parents acceptable behaviour and how to be a member of a community. They do this by word and by deed. A child will watch how dad behaves at the post office and when he takes his first letter he will mimic dad's ways. From their parents children need to learn social skills and gender specific skills.

To feel he belongs

It is a frightened and lonely boy who gets pushed off the football team and ostracised from his peer group. If he is loved and valued at home he is halfway to dealing with this difficult situation. With help, direction and support he needs to learn how to handle this. For mental health he needs a secure position within his family, and in his peer group which will eventually include his work place.

To feel valued

For mental health, we need to feel we have value. Some parents have an expectancy that children know how to behave and will ignore good behaviour. When children misbehave they will react with anger and therefore teach children with negative reinforcement. To get parent attention, children will learn to misbehave. If parents are always angry a child will feel little value.

Children need to know that they have an intrinsic importance; that by the very nature of being human, they have value. They can learn that all human life has value, and that means that they, too, have automatic value.

To be a valuable member of their group they can feel value in the group. When they have a specific role it gives them social value. For example a solicitor has particular value, as does a bricklayer or teacher. Those are easily accepted by our social group. Some are not so clearly defined but we all have value. It is helpful if we feel value within ourselves. Parents can foster that.

Children need *positive reinforcement* when they have done things well, and *careful non-punitive direction* if they get things wrong. They need to learn about reward for effort. They need to learn that when they do something wrong, that it is not he who is bad but his actions. This way a child can grow up valuing himself.

Unconditional Acceptance

This one is very important. We need to be accepted by those who love us, unconditionally. For mental health we need to know that we have a right to our life which has value in the eyes of another. Loved ones are our mirror and without it we become invisible. Mature parents instinctively love us. As we outgrow out families we will replace them with friends and hopefully attach ourselves to someone who will also love us and accept us unconditionally.

To learn the life skills to make him independent

Teaching independence can start early. In small doses and at age appropriate times children are capable of learning and understanding that they will eventually stand alone. If a little boy wants to be a policeman or fireman when he is four it is not a good time to alert him to the dangers of these vocations. At this stage he wants to learn to be a useful man and test his little body to its fighting limits. He will want to be a 'goodie' and fight off 'baddies' as he will want to practice protecting his space and the people he loves, and will quite naturally make swords and guns to help him with his battles. When he is older and more able to see the destructive implications of these you can take him by the hand and have that discussion. Warning him too early will create a problem for him which is bigger then a solution he can understand and will induce guilt and fear and may sow early seeds of anxiety.

And finally, it is your job to teach him to recognise when it is time to leave home. Many parents struggle with this one, and find it difficult to push their child out of the proverbial nest. It is, however, part of their remit even if the reluctant offspring makes it unpleasant. Children have many unwitting strategies to make things easy for themselves and stay put. If they are still home well past the time when it is reasonable for them to set up on their own, then you have missed a trick and have work to do.

Missed a bit
Perfect parenting does not exist, and your parents may have missed out on any of the good parenting practices needed to give you a good start. Generally, parents do their best and they will likely have wanted the best for you.

When you reach adulthood, your life is your responsibility. Your parents are no longer responsible for you. It is then up to you to take stock and see what's left for you to do. You have options. You can blame, shame or carry resentments. These will make life unpleasant for you.

There are options whereby you can help yourself. You just need to get creative and use what skills, methods and talents you do have to get your body and mind to health and happiness.

You have one life to live. How do you want to live it? It's up to you now!

SECTION TWO

Psychological Disturbances and Disorders

Section 2 gives insight into some psychological disturbances and disorders. It uses illustrated examples of why some people behave the way they do, and may give the reader an understanding of how behaviour is influenced by circumstances, and the way a person's programmed script is acted out.

Chapter Six
PSYCHOLOGICAL DISTURBANCES: SPOILED – ANGRY – HOOLIGAN

We often wonder why some people 'go off the rails'. We worry that this could happen to any of us; and worse that it could happen to our children. We wonder why some youngsters are so angry. We may wonder why some people seem so different. There is still much that psychology does not understand about human behaviour but there is also much we do know.

In this chapter we will try to understand why healthy children become disturbed adults and that generally they are predictably living out their script sometimes as a result of learned behaviour.

A SPOILT CHILD

There is no such thing as a naughty child – just uninformed parenting. If a child acts as a classic spoilt child; that is if he shouts or stomps his feet or swears at you to get his way and then gets it, then that is what he has learned and what works for him. It is his job to move forward and if that's how you have let him move forward then you haven't done him any favours. Believe me, a spoilt child is not a happy child. He is probably quite a frightened child. How is it that his parents have allowed him so much control? He is too young to be in charge.

Sometimes parents can find themselves in a position where the child rules the roost and have no idea how to change it anymore. It wasn't so bad when he was small and giving in was easier then facing the challenge. For all children who naturally adapt themselves to their environment they will think this is normal. "I want something and if I shout loud enough I will get it." This means he has no clear boundaries in which to develop. He can't sit and play quietly in a learning environment because there is so much around he can demand to have that he has little time to concentrate on any one area of growth.

Life goes on and he gets bigger and more demanding. This is normal now until he gets to playgroup. He's used to having his way and starts to take things from other children. The group leaders soon put him right and he learns with great pain that in the outside world the rules are different. So now he adapts himself to what he has learned. At home he is in charge but outside he is not. As he gets older and visits friends he sees that other children don't have so much control at home and begins to feel that something isn't right. Why don't his friends have to shout and scream at their parents to get what they need? Mum, dad, what's going on? But the pay-off is too tempting and our spoilt child wants his material goods. All he has to do is demand to have them and his parents give in. It's a system that works but something doesn't feel right. His self-respect is not really in tact. His respect for his parents is not quite right. "Mum, dad, please take charge. I'm only a child!"

Meanwhile, the parents are feeling a similar frustration. Giving in is now running out of control and the battles start. Most often the battles end up between the parents and in the end, for a quiet life one of them relents. The demands get bigger and there is misery all around.

IT'S NOT TOO LATE
It's never too late to change that.

Ben is seventeen and learning to drive. He says to his father coming home from work, "dad, I want you to take me out for a driving lesson now". Dad is tired and knows he has a lot of paper work that evening but Ben usually gets what he wants. Mother says "Oh, go on. You know he's dying to get his licence, and you'll be home before dinner". Dad feels his usual frustration and long term anger at yet again having no control over his own life.

So what can he do? He may need help for this. He needs to understand that it is not healthy for his child to have so much control. He needs to discuss this with his wife and she too needs to understand, if not for her sake then for the sake of her husband and son. He can then say, "Son, I'm tired and I don't have time tonight". For Ben this is irritating as he will now have to deal with this in his usual learned fashion. He will raise his voice and demand dad takes him driving. But something is different today. Father repeats calmly that he will not go today as he is tired and has no time. He says, "I love you son and I know this is important to you, however, I am your father and a reasonable adult, and will happily take you another time, but not tonight". Oh dear.

Now in full battle regalia Ben shouts and swears and kicks the kitchen table. His father calmly asks him "why does that make you so angry"? Ben argues with great anger his reason for his fury but nothing coherent comes out as he doesn't really know himself. He rants and raves but he has never had to draw out his demands to a logical conclusion. His father sticks firmly to his decision and Ben eventually calms down. They negotiate a future time for a driving lesson and the family has dinner together. Ben is aware that there is a new regime in the family dynamic and sleeps well that night.

Since then Ben still makes demands but father makes the final decisions. Eventually Ben begins negotiating with his father in a more mature fashion and father and son have learned to respect each other.

If a spoilt child reaches adulthood without such resolution, he will want to find a partner who will give in to his unreasonable demands and may harbour a deep resentment towards them for not rescuing him from himself just like his parents didn't. This will perpetuate a painful frustration.

Not to be confused with the Pampered child.

The pampered child has different problems. He has others do for him what he could do for himself.[10] Once this skill is learned he will use whatever strategies he can find to maintain that position and why not. Who would give that up? When he outgrows the family he will surround himself with sufficient helpers and rescuers to maintain his comfortable life as by now he hasn't any experience doing things for himself at home. There are always plenty of those around who need to feel needed for the pampered people. He may never need to take responsibility for his life. That's just as well as he's had no training. Future relationships will be hard.

ANGRY CHILDREN

ANDREW'S STORY

When Andrew was a boy, he was a happy child; well behaved and a credit to his parents. He and his little brother and his mum and dad were close and did a lot together. His parents were quite strict and because Andrew was the eldest he had little space to do anything unseen. His parents were good people who monitored their children carefully and wanted the best for them. In trying to protect them from harm they gave their children little room to explore, take risks and make mistakes.

For Andrew, this was a bit stifling, but he noticed many of his friends were in the same boat and, although often frustrated, he mostly got on with it and did what his parents expected of him. Occasionally, Andrew managed to try something unbeknown to his parents.

One evening after the 'battle of the bands', he and some friends went for a drink, tried some lager, and smoked cigarettes. When he got home his father smelled the alcohol on his breath and hit the roof. Andrew was grounded for a month and made to feel like he was a lawless criminal. Andrew found it both confusing and humiliating that his father was so upset with him. He loved his parents and didn't want to upset them, but he also felt a deep need to explore his world. Something wasn't right. When he tried explaining this to his dad, his dad reacted with great anger and the discussion seemed futile.

Andrew felt huge frustration. He was so angry with his dad for not listening to him and for not understanding. He was confused about his own need to go out and try new things. He was angry with his own needs. "Oh, why does it have to be so difficult?"

Life went on and Andrew learned how to behave to keep his parents happy but felt a constant grumbling restlessness working its way under his normal day to day behaviour. Soon Andrew was ready to go to University. Typically, he was both nervous and excited and wondered what lay ahead. Mum and dad got him settled into halls and Andrew soon got on with Uni life. His parents were often on the phone to him and Andrew learned to tell them what they wanted to hear and got on with things.

As he was now not under constant surveillance, he spent a lot of time on the computer and found out he could play some games that earned him some money to pay for his beer and cigarettes. Sometimes he lost money and then he would feel anxious. He learned that smoking some 'weed' helped reduce his anxiety and soon lessons drifted into the background and games and smoking featured more heavily. He knew his circumstances were not good, but kept putting off dealing with things until it was too late.

Andrew and his parents had a hard lesson to learn. Because Andrew was never encouraged to become independent and learn, in small doses to manage his own life, he had no experience of mature behaviour on his own.

His parents blamed Andrew and deep down felt they failed him somehow and had to come to terms with that. Where did it all go wrong? How could their perfect family fall apart so badly? Andrew felt a great anger with himself and with his parents and moved somewhere far away. He felt his parents were good people so it must all be his fault that things went wrong and developed a deep loathing for himself. He lost himself in drugs. It was years before he visited his family and resolved their feelings.

Anger is an unhealthy state of mind. It can precipitate many physical diseases. It is an emotion designed to be used occasionally to protect us from enemies and gathers up all available strength to deal with a life or death situation. It is hard on the body and needs to be recovered from. Placing yourself in a perceived state of danger and experiencing constant anger is destructive and unhealthy and much better sorted.

If you as parents are the enemy then it is time to see that it may be your immaturity that is stopping everyone from growing. If parents place an invisible wall in front of a child, he will sit there stuck and frustrated. How can he recognise it as a barrier and understand that it is your limitations that are blocking his development? He will blame himself and perhaps never understand where his frustration came from. If he is creative he will find help and move on that way. If he is offered comfort from drugs or alcohol he may settle for that.

HOOLIGANISM

Hooliganism is a new disease in society and Britain has one of the largest hooligan populations in modern Europe. What is it all about? For most of us it's a social phenomenon that we don't completely understand but we feel sure that the people involved must be undisciplined youngsters who only need a firm hand or a good clip around the ear to make them model citizens.

MARK'S STORY

Mark is 14 years old. Mark has an older brother and two younger brothers and a little sister. Mark's parents both work hard to earn enough money to pay for their home, food and what luxuries they can afford. There is very little time for communication within the family; therefore, often it is easier for the parents to shout instructions to the children rather then take the time to explain things. When the children are arguing it is easier for the parents to order them to stop then to see that Mark is being bullied by his older brother.

Somehow there is an expectation that the children automatically know what to do and how to behave, and any naughty behaviour is often reinforced with loads of negative attention. Good behaviour is the expectation and therefore good behaviour is largely ignored.

Mark often feels misunderstood. In order to feel alive, he will do whatever he needs to get his parents' attention and to be noticed. As Mark grows up needing parent recognition he will get their attention even as a result of bad behaviour as 'even the bad love is better then no love'. This is what he is now most familiar with. Unfortunately, this type of attention is now programming him to believe he is worthless, inadequate and a bad person. Mark is now carrying a lot of pain which has been insidiously growing inside him since he was very young.

Mark feels quite miserable now. Every time these days when his parents speak to him they seem angry with him. He gets angry back. By this time it has become habit more then anything else as no one has ever modelled kindness to him or shown him the approval that a child needs in order to thrive. Mark cannot understand why everyone is always so cross with him. Where is the respect? Where is the human dignity?

He goes out and kicks his football. He and his mates dream about becoming rich and famous football players which will give him the social adulation he so badly needs because the older he gets and the more he is made to feel worthless, the more he needs to believe he will one day have this. Many times he will feel how hopeless this is and feel unhappy.

He knows deep down he's a great person. Why can't his mum and dad see this? Why is this not being reinforced by the two people whose love and approval he needs more then anything else? He is angry with his parents. His anger makes him kick his football hard. He is now firmly convinced that "they don't care about me – why should I care about them". His ball smashes Mr. Jones' window. Now Mr. Jones and his parents are angry. More people come and they are all angry. Mark feels terrible. "Why is everyone always so angry?" he wonders. "I'll show them". Now, depending on Mark's temperament it will

COUNSELLING D I Y – Understanding Mental Health

determine how much retribution there will be for a society which has let him down so badly.

If his favourite role model, his father, modelled to him when he was a child that it's okay to laugh when dad broke something of a neighbour's, then he has permission to laugh at Mr. Jones and his broken window as well, even though dad may now be quite cross.

Mark spends more and more time with his friends who also have angry parents. They begin to feel that there is no pleasing parents, so let's just please ourselves. In fact, the grown-ups have let us down so badly, let's see how we can hurt them back. We can be really naughty and fuel that anger with alcohol which will dilute any feelings of guilt or remorse we may feel, and further insult the adult world by taking the illegal drugs which will allow us to be even less inhibited and more destructive.

We are the angry children who have been let down by the people who were supposed to protect us and love us unconditionally. Let's see what mischief we can get up to at the football stadium, a place where dad and I had some good times.

To the extreme this could lead to psychopathy, now known as Anti-social Personality Disorder.

Chapter Seven
EATING DISORDERS

ANOREXIA NERVOSA

Tracy is 15 and anorexic. Whenever she looked at herself in the mirror she grimaced and would then lie on her bed, listen to her favourite music, look at her magazine and wonder why she couldn't look like the models before her. Tracy was underweight but no matter how hard she tried, the image grimacing back at her in the mirror was always bigger and fatter then she wished. She sighed. Something was bothering Tracy but she wasn't sure what. She just felt depressed.

Tracy's family was a close, loving family who did a lot together. Sometimes, Tracy felt they were too close. For as long as she could remember mum was always on a diet and constantly involving the whole family in her fastidious beliefs in good eating habits. Tracy's older sister and younger brothers mostly just ignored mum when she talked about diets and got on with their lives. Tracy hated mealtimes.

Tracy's mum knew exactly what everyone in the household ate and watched them carefully. In fact Tracy's mum seemed to know everything about everyone's business in the family and had an opinion about it. Poor old dad was kept up to date and made to enforce her rules by monitoring schoolwork, bedtimes, and everyone's comings and goings. Tracy had little say in things.

The term Anorexia Nervosa[11] actually means 'nervous loss of appetite', yet most anorexics may continue to have a strong pre-occupation with food. The diagnostic criteria for anorexia are:

i   The individual maintains a body weight which is below the average expected body weight (AEBW) according to age, sex and height.

ii   There is a disturbance in the way the individual sees him/herself in terms of weight, size and shape. They generally see themselves or parts of themselves as fat.

iii   He or she has an intense fear of becoming 'fat' despite the fact that they are underweight.

iv   In women there needs to be an absence of at least three consecutive menstrual cycles.

Anorexia has a fatal outcome in 5 – 10% of diagnosed cases, a higher rate then for any other psychological disorder. It is often accompanied by symptoms of prolonged starvation such as stopping of menstruating, slow heart rate, low body temperature, high blood pressure, tummy pains and/or lanugo, which is the appearance of fine body hair.

These days Tracy hardly eats at all. She has recently been diagnosed anorexic and mum is worried. She tries her best to get Tracy to eat something. She tries gentle persuasion, firm lectures, cooking Tracy's favourite meals but Tracy won't eat.

Anorexia is often a way for young girls and sometimes boys to have some control over their lives. It is a way to deal with an anxiety they have that something doesn't feel right in their perception of themselves or their world, which may be perfectly acceptable to someone else.

Children need respect and as they become teens they need some privacy. They will need some autonomy in their lives, areas where they slowly start to take charge of their own destiny without fear of scrutiny and living up to others' expectations. In recognising this they can be helped to understand that there may be an underlying anxiety which they are trying to deal with. With support they can look at what it is which is causing their anxiety in a way which is not so damaging to their health.

BULIMIA NERVOSA

Cassandra was a happy-go-lucky child who enjoyed her food and it was quite simply a fact that 'Sandy' was always a little on the chubby side. As she grew older Sandy started to take more interest in her appearance but also enjoyed her second helping of chips and tomato sauce, especially accompanied with fresh bread and thick butter. Yum! Mother didn't like confrontation and easily gave in.

As a young teenager Sandy worked hard at looking smart and watched her friends and tried watching her lunches, and the more she tried the harder it got. Many evenings she would feel low and just think, "It is too difficult" and comfort herself with thick slices of bread and butter and jam, but afterwards feel huge remorse, wishing desperately she could be as thin as her friends. She would get very cross with herself.

One day she made herself vomit up her lovely feast of bread, butter and jam. "There, that feels better. No more guilt." But something clicked in her mind. "I can do that again and have the best of both worlds." She now had a way of eating what she wanted but be unaffected by the calories. She could now eat so much that it hurt. Slowly it became a secret habit; one which became invasive and hard to control.

Bulimia Nervosa is the condition of binge-eating and then purging. Bulimia literally means 'ox hunger' and has only been recognised as separate from Anorexia Nervosa since the 70's. Bulimia Nervosa usually begins in late adolescence or early adult life.[12] The binge eating frequently begins during or after an episode of dieting. Disturbed eating patterns persist for at least several years in a high percentage of clinic samples.

Psychologically, this is as a result of an ego which has not properly matured in this area. It was not taught in small doses during critical times of its life to take control of itself and then feel the rewards of that such as parent approval; or getting the bike with saved pocket money; or seeing parents making mature decisions with happy outcomes. Then the internal superego says to the ever demanding id "there, there; of course you can eat the cake if you want it". Once sated, the id then demands to be thin and the super-ego finds the solution, purging. There is no mature ego to take charge of this continuous see-saw.

Vomiting is the most common method of purging and is used by 80 or 90% of bulimic individuals.[13] The immediate effects of vomiting are that it brings relief from the physical discomfort of over eating, and reduces the fear of weight gain. Other methods of purging include the misuse of laxatives and diuretics.

Symptoms of Bulimia are:

i.   recurrent episodes of binge eating (rapid consumption of food in a discrete period of time)

ii.   a feeling of lack of control over eating behaviour during these binges.

iii.   self-induced vomiting, use of laxatives or diuretics, strict dieting or fasting, or vigorous exercise

iv.   at least 2 binge episodes a month for 3 months

v.   over concern with body shape and weight

Recurrent vomiting may lead to metabolic disturbances, especially hypocalcaemia (low calcium levels) which can leave the person feeling very weak. It can often affect dental enamel, particularly of the front teeth, which may begin to appear ragged and 'moth-eaten'. To the extreme, it can cause an electrolyte imbalance which can lead to death.

Bulimia has been reported to occur all over the world. At least 90% of bulimics are female and is often associated with some forms of depression with an increased frequency of depressive symptoms such as low self-esteem; anxiety disorders such as fear of social situations; or mood disturbances in individuals with bulimia. These mood and anxiety disturbances are frequently helped following effective treatment of the condition. With help and over longer term follow up, the symptoms of many individuals appear to diminish.

OBESITY

Carla is a married mum with two young children. Carla loves being a parent and enjoys all the activities that go with it. She walks Matthew to school each morning and she and Katy wave him off as Katy clambers back in her push chair and they sing 'Postman Pat' all the way home.

Carla has always been heavy but since the children were born Carla has put on a lot of weight. She is now up to 14 stone, a lot of weight to carry for her 5'4" frame. She keeps meaning to go on a diet but each time she tries she can't do it. Summer was coming and this time she was determined to shed some pounds. She bought cottage cheese and lots of fruit and made a chart, but when she was making chips and fish fingers for the children's tea she began what was by now a familiar debate in her mind. "Why can't I have any chips? It's not fair"; and deep feelings of emotional neglect and denial cause Carla so much pain that she needed to console that awful emptiness in herself. She just could not think about her future or her resolve.

There is inside Carla a very frightened little girl who needs comfort and who has never learned that there is reward for making mature decisions; that is, making decisions which don't just give immediate gratification but also long term rewards. She has never learned how to make mature decisions which benefits the individual and/or the larger group in the long run. The smell of chips is now overwhelming and Carla gives in. Chances are if someone had tried to stop her she might have felt quite angry with them because her need was so great. Anger is, after all, a mask for pain.

The human body is a marvellous machine and converts tasty food into energy. If we eat more then what we burn off it neatly distributes it as stored energy in the form of fat all around the body. Any more and it likes to find an easily portable area such as the mid region or thighs for storing and future use. However, great excesses can lead to problems as the body and its organs strain to hang on to it. We then have no choice but to ask ourselves what our need is to store such dangerous amounts of fat.

Psychologically speaking, a part of Carla's ego is not mature. Perhaps, as a child Carla never learned or was rewarded for making difficult decisions. This may have been as a result of her parenting or maybe her own perception of being denied.

Perhaps she never needed to make decisions because a parent or sibling made them for her. Perhaps there were few rewards. As she was too young to be aware of her needs at the time, she only has a woolly, uncomfortable feeling about it now, unsure of what is wrong.

As part of the maturing process, or ego development children need to learn to make small decisions for which the reward is parent approval, the most important reward for a thriving ego, so that eventually the growing mind can take care of itself. The brain with constantly growing neuron development is then also adapted to this new found skill and can then grow accordingly. If a child has not learned this in childhood and the adaptive brain has not incorporated this in its memory bank then it will be difficult to make it up as an adult. It is hard to put a good structure on a rocky foundation.

Obese people tend to eat high energy food at night. It is then difficult to burn it off and the energy converts to fat. There has been a lot of hypothesis over the years to explain what factors contribute to obesity. Occasionally, hormonal disturbances such as hyperinsulinemia can produce overeating and obesity.[14] It is also believed that for some the senses are more stimulated by external factors. Also, for some people the metabolism doesn't burn off the energy intake as quickly as others, as in Prader-Willi syndrome.[15] Stress and anxiety can also lead to overeating as it brings compensatory rewards and pleasure. Many experts believe there is a co-relation between obesity and low self esteem.

There may be many psychological reasons for holding the weight. For some, it means they have tagged themselves unattractive and therefore don't have to compete in the world of fashion or being 'cool'. For others it may mean they will be ignored and not so visible on the world stage. For others still it means they have chosen to be sexually unattractive and others won't be interested in them sexually. For many however it is more to do with the comfort of eating and needing the external solace to make up for an inner emptiness.

Life is hard for obese people in our society. They really do need help, so that they can themselves understand that for them it is difficult to take charge of their diet. Just like when we learn a second language it is learned with a different part of the brain as the first language, an obese person can learn to understand their eating habits by accessing different learning to override what to them is a natural compulsion to eat in order to comfort great pain from within. Just like diabetics or people with physical disabilities have to learn to live with their disability, so too does a person suffering from obesity have to come to grips with their disability if they want to take charge of their lives.

Chapter Eight
CLINICAL DEPRESSION

JAKE'S STORY

Jake is fourteen. Jake wanted a pair of designer jeans for the end of term party to impress his friends, particularly the girls, however his parents said they couldn't afford them and Jake had to settle for ordinary, less expensive jeans. Jake's parents said they couldn't see what the problem was as the new jeans looked great. Jake felt depressed. Not only could he not present himself to his friends looking as cool as he felt he deserved to look but his parents just didn't understand.

Jake's depression is short-lived but real. It is a frustration which has no where to go. Depending on Jake's history and temperament, it will determine how deep the feeling goes. Most probably he would be fine with a resulting determination that just as soon as he's old enough he will get a job to earn enough money to buy the jeans he needs to feel good. He has an outlet.

JENNY'S STORY

Jenny's story is different. Jenny's dad worked in a big office which he loved. Jenny's mum got quite frustrated that dad spent so much time at the office and felt resentful. She would take that out on Jenny and her baby brother, Bart. Mum always seemed sad or upset and Jenny didn't understand. No matter how hard Jenny tried, she couldn't get mum interested in her, or what she did.

When a child feels disapproved of or finds it difficult to please her carers she can become frustrated and have feelings of anger. Depending on how early in her life she becomes consciously or unconsciously aware of this, it may set up a life long sense of feeling inadequate. She may feel a constant frustration that no matter how hard she tries, she feels she is just not good enough, and eventually begins to believe it. No matter how hard she tries, and how angry she gets, she just cannot get the important people in her life to love her and approve of her. Being the adaptive animal she is she tries every strategy available to her, including crying, cuddling, being naughty, being nice, etc. It seems futile. Eventually the anger has no where to go and just turns inwards. She becomes lethargic. She tries to get on with her life and with her friends and on the surface all looks well but something doesn't feel right.

By the time Jenny reaches adulthood she may feel she is always on the outside, looking in. She also feels that she is not appreciated or seen as good enough by her friends, or future partner, or by her employers.

This may be the onset of clinical depression.[16] The slightest knock to her confidence now makes her depressed. She has no historical life experience of 'snapping out of it' and boosting her own mood as she never learned how as a child. She has little or no experience of being happy. She may replace this with artificial 'feel good' things such as smoking or drinking alcohol, or whatever she learned over her life which gave her some personal pleasure, but somehow, these never quite replaced the empty feeling she experiences much of the time. Without the experience of unconditional love and approval during her early years she is not equipped to deal with her sadness. Depending on her personal character and temperament it remains to be seen how deep her depression will go. She is lacking a good foundation of self-esteem to give her the personal strength from which to draw on in times of need.

There is to date no proven reason why some people suffer from depression but history points strongly to coping strategies learned in early childhood and the development of a positive sense of self.

We have all experienced feelings of sadness or irritability, or felt fed up and will say that we are feeling depressed. If our favourite football team looses then we may say that we are depressed or if we hear bad news we can say that that is depressing. These are normal feelings we all have from time to time. Such feelings, however, can help us understand and can give us a little insight into real, clinical depression. Clinical depression is broadly divided into two categories; *reactive* depression and *endogenous* depression.

REACTIVE DEPRESSION
Reactive depression, as the name suggests, is usually a reaction to a circumstance. For example, bereavement, or moving from a familiar community, or the break-up of a marriage can cause great pain and leave a person feeling deeply depressed. The difference in reactive depression is that a person knows why they are depressed and they can, therefore, make some sense of it. A person can then generally tell you why they are depressed and more readily talk about it, which helps recovery. Reactive depression can be intense or more manageable. For example, if Danny lived with his single mother well into his adulthood, and she suddenly became ill and died, it is understandable that Danny would feel lost without his mother who was his world and that he should become very depressed. This would be a deeper depression then the young man who moved away from home and is not so intensely affected in his day to day life by the absence of his mother.

Feeling Displaced
If a person was happy in her familiar community and was suddenly uprooted, it wouldn't surprise anyone that this person may become deeply despondent and depressed. In time, however, and with a positive attitude, these kinds of depressions may be overcome.

Reactive Depression is characterised by the following symptoms:

- person generally knows why they are depressed
- disturbed sleep but more problematic at night as the person may lay awake with worrying and negative thoughts

- no self-motivation but friends and activities may be helpful

- often as a result of circumstance, including bereavement, moving home, divorce, failure to achieve, pressure or stress, unresolved issues, etc.

Reactive Depression is a normal reaction to sad circumstances. We are creatures of habit and a sudden change in familiar lifestyle is difficult. In time and with the support of friends and family, a person can adapt to the new circumstances and eventually find happiness when the new life becomes familiar and reliable. Talking about your pain helps you share and thereby dilute the intensity of it. If friends or family are unavailable, then counselling is a good option, and sometimes even better as you can then fully concentrate on your needs in a facilitating environment.

ENDOGENOUS (OR BIOLOGICAL) DEPRESSION

Endogenous Depression has no clear root and can happen to a person anytime. There is no particular trigger for this debilitating condition and it can just seem to start from nowhere. The word '*endogenous*' means 'coming from within'. The current belief is that it may be as a result of having a pre-disposition to depression which may have been learned in infancy or early childhood. For example, if a mother is suffering from post natal depression and has little or no support, her baby will undoubtedly be affected. Baby will not be picked up as much as she perhaps needs, or cuddled or embraced. It is likely she will not experience as much love and pride from her mother as a baby who has a happy, supported mum.

Her mood may not appear as depression until she becomes an adult, when deep feelings of pain or inadequacies may come out. She may rifle through her early programming looking for direction and find only sad memories and no happy experiences for herself, or to pass on to her baby. Her unconscious will not know contentedness, and may hold deep feelings of unsupported anxieties. A baby raised by a depressed mum may not feel as secure when she grows up as a baby whose mum is excited about motherhood and her new baby. If a baby is raised in an atmosphere where parents are unhappy with each other, then she may also pick up feelings of insecurity. Like these examples, there are any number of circumstances which could result in leaving baby with deep rooted feelings of inadequacy or insecurity which may result in clinical depression. Baby's personal character will determine how much she will be affected.

Endogenous depression is characterised by the following symptoms.

- early waking and difficulty in going back to sleep
- feel hopeless about themselves and the future
- overwhelming sense of emptiness and misery
- difficulty concentrating
- neglect personal hygiene
- lack of motivation
- general loss of interest in everything

Endogenous depression is difficult to cope with but in time, and with understanding why it is there, it is possible to turn it around. By facing the deep hurt inside and accepting that it is not your fault you can start to give yourself permission to be happy. Find out what things you enjoy doing and then start doing them. By looking after your inner child and giving her the love she so badly needs, you can rescue her and the wounded adult she has become. You have as much right to be happy as anyone else so get out there and pamper yourself a little and keep busy. You need to re-learn how to be happy if you want a piece of what's rightfully as much yours as anyone's – contented happiness.

Sometimes, for endogenous depression, the support of a counsellor for an extended period of time can be very healing.

POST NATAL DEPRESSION

Mums are very important people. In the great scheme of things they mostly take on the responsibility of raising the children and ultimately, the next generation. Mum has a strong instinct to want the best for her children and has a big influence on their behaviour, how her children will feel about themselves, and how they see their futures. She knows this and has taken on this task to fulfil her baby's and her own deep needs. She quite happily makes many personal sacrifices on her baby's behalf. She has a job to do and she does it.

It is important that she feels good about herself and what she is doing. She is educated, organised and intelligent. She has a fairly realistic idea about married life and parenthood and now spends much of her energy trying to make these a reality. As she knows how much her baby needs her, she is quite prepared to put her own needs last as she gets on with the huge task of motherhood.

However, what she hasn't banked on is how tired she is. This will vary for all new mums but be fair; your body has just been through a phenomenally traumatic birth experience. It is working hard through triggered stimulus to restore itself to good post natal health not to mention manufacturing breast milk for nurturing your new baby. Both, your body and your mind need plenty of rest and support to cope with this.

If mum doesn't get enough rest, the body reacts by lowering levels of chemicals in the body as it struggles with making sufficient fuel to support body and breast milk. After all, nature says that a helpless baby's needs come first. This may result in reduced levels of the hormone, dopamine and may cause depression. Mum starts to feel low. 'Baby blues' which often show up shortly after birth is quite common and can be as a result of the physiological anti-climax of hormones and chemicals trying to restore balance in your body. This may result in uncharacteristic bouts of crying or angry outbursts. But these feelings soon go as mum gets herself and baby into a new routine.

Extra rest can help this process along. A tired new mum will struggle without adequate rest. She may feel tearful and less in control. Her self esteem may be affected and she becomes unsure of herself. For the sake of her baby, and also her need to keep order in her life she may push herself and become even more tired. Without an adequately nutritious diet, she has even less chance of building up her strength. Without her partner's or family's support she may become exhausted.

Now what's going to happen? A seeping, insidious frustration starts to creep in. A tired mum's mind will try to make sense of what she is feeling, but the more tired she gets the more primitive her feelings and her logic become. Her usual mature ego will give way to less mature feelings of meeting her more primitive needs of safety and security. If her partner can't help because he is working long hours to secure more money to pay for his increased family costs; and family are living miles away, then things can go wrong. Feelings of frustration can give rise to a futile helplessness with no solution in sight. She may think "everyone is coping – what's wrong with me". Frustration and anger have no where else to go and become internalised. This may be the early stages of depression as she toils endlessly to cover up her feelings of inadequacy.

Depression is when a person feels overwhelmed by feelings of helplessness, hopelessness and sadness.

She may look for someone to blame. Will it be baby, her absent family or partner, or herself? Whatever happens, life is not fun anymore. There is no balance. The amount of unhappiness far outweighs the good bits. This may be the onset of post-natal depression. This happens to at least 10% - 20% of new mums.

Regardless of how you deal with post natal depression, both you and baby are bound to be affected. It can be an extremely difficult time for both of you. The worst thing is that it is hard to ask for help as you may be feeling low and inadequate, so you battle on and feel even worse.

Baby will now be sensing your sadness and may be affected by feeling insecure and cry more then usual. If this carries on for an extended period of time then baby's development can't help but be affected. He will now be absorbing messages of feeling depressed. He will be learning how to feel depressed himself. Let's see what's going on with baby.

Firstly he is not having the experience of growing in a secure environment. This may result in him never knowing how that may feel and therefore he will not be able to recreate that for his future babies. This is now part of his early programming.

Secondly, he cannot spend all his energy moving forward as he does not feel particularly safe and needs to spend energy protecting himself. Neurological development will be affected because who wants to learn when you're feeling unsafe. That means his brain isn't taking up all the opportunities for growth. His energy is needed elsewhere. Because he is too young to understand exactly what's going on, he just spends it feeling somewhat miserable and cries more.

Thirdly, what he does have is experience of a depressed carer and may feel the projected depression in himself. This may lead to a future pre-disposition to becoming depressed; a sad legacy to pass on to your child. This may be the reason why you are feeling so low if you have experience of a depressed mum or carer during your early years.

By instinct, baby knows he needs to feel safe. With confident and caring handling baby can happily settle in to a pattern of healthy growth and lets you know by behaving in a contented manner. Unless there is a physical problem with baby he will reward confident parenting with contentedness. This way nature provides for him an environment for healthy development.

If mum feels she has post-natal depression or is clinically depressed it would be most helpful for both her and her baby to seek help. If not, then her depression may affect baby long term and a deep sense of insecurity could stay with baby for a very long time.

Chapter Nine
ANXIETY DISORDERS

GENERAL ANXIETY

TOBY'S STORY

Toby and his mum with his sister in a push chair were learning to cross the road and to look both ways to get across safely. Great! Toby's brain would register the new life skill programming and all should be well. While they were crossing the road, Toby accidentally dropped his pencil and ran back to pick it up. Mum shrieked with horror and severely admonished Toby telling him how he was responsible for nearly killing all of them. By the time she had dealt with her hysteria Toby's brain had registered severe anxiety with some trauma. Some children may cope with that but for others it will sow seeds for future anxiety.

If mum had calmed down and immediately apologised and reassured Toby it wasn't his fault and that she should not have got so cross it could have undone any damage. She could have talked him through how to handle dropped pencils in the road. Then Toby would have felt better. Reassurance and crossing the road again properly would then have resolved the issue and diffused his anxiety. There is then a balance between perceived danger and real danger. Trauma is perceived danger fused in the brain.

Anxiety needs diffusing. We all know that if you fall off a bike or a horse you need get straight back on again. If you are hurt you need some comforting before you get back on again. With a reassuring helper it is easier. With a cuddle and some soothing words dad will help him back on his bike or mum will help her back on her horse. We have then recognised there may be danger but with reassurance can then learn to deal with the fear. We can make the mature decision that accidents happen and with care these can be minimized. The id has had a fright, the superego has alerted you to the dangers and with help the ego has learned to manage a mature outcome. The fear has not turned into anxiety.

When a person seeks counselling for anxiety it is the ego which needs support. Counselling then recognises perceived fears and the long haul of diffusing anxiety can begin. Undoing psychological disturbances can sometimes take a very long time.

KATE'S STORY

Kate is shy. It is her first day at secondary school. Her best friend from primary school has chosen to go elsewhere and Kate is feeling very nervous on her own. Her new tie and blazer are making her feel awkward, and two boys who just passed her going in the opposite direction had started laughing. Were they laughing at her?

It's probably safe to say that Kate's stress level is high. Her palms are likely to be sweaty and her face is pale. Her heart is beating faster then normal and her muscles are tense. Her mouth is dry and she feels slightly dizzy. She steps into her form room with trepidation and carefully glances around. She spots a girl she knows who has an empty seat next to her. They smile at one another and both feel enormously relieved to see someone familiar. Soon Kate's stress symptoms diminish and she begins to feel normal and safe again.

The emotion, stress, is housed in the limbic system, the old part of the brain where emotions are stored and which had prepared Kate for 'fight or flight' in order to protect her. She was in a new and unfamiliar place and her body was ready to deal with impending danger. When it was clear there was none her body relaxed.

Stress is necessary and common in our day to day life. It keeps us safe from harm and helps protect us from danger. It prepares our bodies for action with a rush of adrenalin and makes our senses extra alert to danger. Most of the time we are not even aware that our bodies react like this but we all know how it feels when we are alone and we hear an unexpected noise.

Our bodies immediately react and prepare for defence. Even if we have to do something like make a presentation in front of the class or colleagues at work, our bodies prepare for fight or flight. Mild levels of stress are normal and help us to do our jobs well and keep us on our psychological toes. If, however, we experience stress too often and it starts to affect our normal lives, then it can lead to anxiety and become a real problem.

Stress happens when the things you are taking on outweigh your ability to cope with them. Often expectations from the boss or pressure from teachers can create high levels of stress. When young people have too much stress in their lives, they look for ways to relieve that. Going home and sharing concerns with family members generally releases stress, and watching television and doing other things can create a distraction that can detoxify stress. If there is no outlet for stress at home then young people will look elsewhere. They will look to their friends for relief by sharing their concerns and seeing how they deal with their problems. Some other ways of dealing with stress and relieving anxiety are drinking alcohol, smoking cigarettes, taking recreational drugs, and eating excess food. These activities provide short term relief, however they can eventually make things worse as they add guilt and debt or addiction to the equation.

Joining clubs or doing sport can be a constructive way of dealing with the effects of stress, by taking the focus off yourself and feeling useful. This way it not only relieves stress but can increase self-esteem leaving the way open to developing maturity. In this case maturity would increase because as you become involved with others you inevitable begin to care for the group and begin making decisions which is in the interest of the group. That is a paradigm for the future. That is then a life skill which will prepare you for working as an effective boss, politician, teacher, parent, etc.

GETTING HELP FOR ANXIETY

CATHERINE'S STORY

Catherine wakes up, draws the curtains, and makes herself a cup of tea. She feels anxious but isn't sure why. She makes the children's lunches and drives them to school and herself to work. She is relieved that the car journey is over but now she has to go into the office. She feels anxious again. Her boss asks to see her and would like her to have the figures he asked for sooner then agreed. She feels anxious. Going home she wonders what to cook for supper and whether her family will complain about her choice. She worries about her children and their lives. There seems to be no break from worrying. When Catherine gets home she pours herself a large glass of wine and leaves the bottle open.

For some, impending danger is always there. Sometimes, it is as a result of a chemical imbalance, but more likely, if in early childhood a person hasn't learned coping strategies to protect themselves from harm, the fight-flight mechanism may be in a constant state of readiness. The body is a magnificent machine and under normal circumstances will react instinctively and involuntarily to do what it needs to protect itself. As is made clear in chapter one of this book, the first five years are important for programming the 'soft ware' or the intelligence to help with this protection. Ideally, two caring parents will create an environment where a child will feel safe and can get on with the business of neurological, biological and psychological development. If either of the carers are themselves anxious the child will sense this. Some will internalise it.

If you don't feel secure, how can your child feel secure? If somehow the baby is placed in a regular state of feeling insecure or perceived danger, and has not been gently reassured that there is no danger then she won't have the experience of feeling safe. Her early programming will tell her to feel danger at all times and that's what she will feel for the rest of her life. That's her normal feeling. She knows it isn't quite right but she has no experience of having reassurances and using coping strategies to feel secure. She trusted you to keep her safe and to help and reassure her when there was threat or danger, even on a small scale with childish perceived dangers. This way she could have grown up feeling safe, but now all she has is this niggling feeling of impending danger. Not much fun.

Misdirected and unmanaged emotions will cause anxiety. The ego, the voice of reason in us, experiences anxiety when it feels too weak to deal with what is perceived to be danger. If in childhood, there was no experience of being consoled when there were accidents; or reassurances when there was confusion then a person is not adequately prepared to deal with these on a grander scale in their future. Anxiety needs diffusing.

To protect itself from anxiety our unmanaged ego needs help and employs unconscious mechanisms called ego defences. See Ego Defences, chapter one.

Stress or Anxiety

Stress is normal and healthy. Stress is what gets us moving and gets jobs done. The good feelings which then result from this balances the chemicals created by such stress and on the whole, there is homeostasis. Sustained stress can lead to anxiety. Anxiety is when the body somatises stress. It is when the body begins to show physiological symptoms as a result of prolonged stress. Stress is the situation. Anxiety is how the body reacts to it. Anxiety is the pathological outcome of stress.

These can include :

a)   problems with getting to sleep

b)   waking in the early hours and not being able to go back to sleep

c)   bouts of crying

d)   agitation or irritability

e)   loss of appetite or increased appetite

and eventually may lead to:

f)   heart palpitations

g)   digestion problems or bowel conditions

h)   skin abnormalities

i)   etc.

With sustained stress which leads to symptoms of anxiety it is time to see your GP. If s/he can find no underlying physiological reasons for your symptoms it may be time to listen to your body and see what it is trying to tell you. It is then likely that something unresolved is bothering you. You need to try to understand what it is that you are not dealing with. These could include unresolved issues from childhood or perhaps it is something to do with your new boss, a situation at home or even a fear of flying to that holiday destination you have booked and are now regretting. Maybe it is something else. Perhaps a friend or professional support can help you get to the bottom of it. You can then make decisions of what you can do about it.

What can I do.
Once you have worked out what it is that is bothering you, you can then make a list of options of how to resolve it. Sometimes it is easy and you simply choose your favourite option and you can get on with your life.

Sometimes it is not so easy. Now comes the tricky bit. Sometimes the solutions look very difficult. Now you have to think hard. For many people this is where it may look impossible. Many will settle for the easy option. It is then important to understand that sometimes we need to push ourselves out of our comfort zone and make the right decision which is the hard one. It may even involve upsetting others or it may mean uncomfortable changes. If handled properly, all changes can be positive events. Even children will adapt to new regimes if it is handled with care. You have one life. How do you want to live it.

Chapter Ten
PANIC ATTACKS, POST TRAUMATIC STRESS DISORDER (PTSD), OBSESSIVE COMPULSIVE DISORDER (OCD) AND PHOBIAS

PANIC ATTACKS

JACK'S STORY

Jack was a decent sort. He was a useful member of his family, helped out where he could, and for leisure, spent a lot of time watching science fiction programs. Jack was quite a shy, sensitive chap and didn't like a lot of attention. He had a few close friends and steered away from crowds. What he absolutely hated was talking in front of a large group and when in his English class at age 12 he had to give a three minute talk about healthy eating he froze. The night before he had tossed and turned and slept a few restless hours and couldn't face his breakfast on the day. His body walked to school on the morning of his 'talk' but his brain was on fire, screaming and running in the opposite direction. He could not see how he could escape his fate.

For his presentation, Jack had to stand in front of the whole class and recite the drivel he had scrawled on a curled up piece of A4. Jenny had just talked convincingly about citrus fruits and their merits and even made the whole class laugh. His turn was next. He got up in front of the class and felt his face going red. He tripped over Jenny's basket of oranges and his paper fell on the floor and slid under the teacher's desk. The whole class was in hysterics. After retrieving his notes, he bravely started his talk but his voice made a crackling sound. He pleadingly looked at the teacher who only stared back at him. The screaming brain won. Jack walked out of the class and hoped never to return. After that, Jack panicked every time he had to address a group of people, no matter how small. Socially his confidence got worse as he got older and panic set in more and more frequently. Jack's life was misery.

Panic is defined as discrete periods of intense fear or discomfort and at least four of the following symptoms need to appear during a panic attack: Dyspnoea (shortness of breath); palpitations or accelerated heart rate; chest pain or discomfort; choking or smothering sensations; dizziness; unsteady feelings or faintness; trembling or shaking; sweating and hot and cold flushes; fear of dying. Many people use avoidance to deal with panic attacks.

We accept that some panic in the form of anxiety is normal and necessary to provide us with a certain level of arousal and alertness in order to complete challenging tasks, and will keep us on our 'psychological toes'. However, too much panic directs energy away from the task and creates unhealthy physical symptoms which are not constructive.

Jack had suffered a 'psychological interruption' during a critical time of his life. What could have been a 'confidence booster' became an emotional wound. Without medicine the wound festered and got worse. To help himself in his adulthood, Jack will need to find opportunities to regain his confidence. Professional support could help Jack identify his problem and give him an opportunity to discuss it and thereby reduce anxiety. He could then see what his options were to deal with it, and decide what he could do. Jack would learn that once he recognised his problem and found out he had options which could help improve his life, the choice is then his to do it.

One option of course is to do nothing and he could then see how that would affect his future. Another way would be to start with addressing small groups. For example, a night class at the local college, where he would contribute to the group about a subject he liked, and get positive recognition from other members of the class. Soon Jack would loose himself in the normality of group interaction and in time, loose the fear.

POST-TRAUMATIC STRESS DISORDER (FUSED ANXIETY)

TOM'S STORY

When Tom had picked up his son from the coast it was late and the weather was terrible. In the driving rain he could barely see where he was going and in the middle of chatting with his son whom he hadn't seen for some months he was suddenly aware he wasn't on the road he should be. It was midnight and black and suddenly before him he saw coming out of nowhere what looked like a bright orange petrol station. Within seconds he realised he was no longer on a road but on a pier and was hurtling towards what he now recognised was a huge, brightly lit transport ship. He braked hard and stopped breathing as he dared hope the car would stop in time. As he felt the wheels curling over the edge of the pier, he knew he hadn't and was heading down into the water. His brain immediately registered that they needed to open a door or window fast as the car's electrics would soon be wet and they would be locked in the car like in a coffin. Water pressure would make it impossible to open anything. In his mind he watched the episode as if in slow motion. He suddenly remembered the roof hatch and with luck it still opened about ten inches before the car hit the water. The moment the car made impact with the water the two men unhooked their seat belts and managed to squeeze through the opening and by some miracle managed to escape.

For a long time afterwards Tom continued to relive the event, both during sleep as nightmares and in his waking hours as flashbacks. Each time he relived the event his body reacted with the same physical symptoms including shaking, chills, heart palpitations and panic. Tom had suffered a trauma.

We all respond to traumatic events differently, depending on our character, temperament, and upbringing. In Tom's case he now suffered from Post-Traumatic Stress Disorder, PTSD. About 20% of people who experience an extreme trauma will develop the disorder.

When there is danger our bodies and minds prepare with a fight/flight reaction, however if the body or mind has no time to prepare and the event catches us off guard, then the event does it's damage and fuses in the brain.

PTSD has been described as a feeling of being in a psychological prison. You desperately want life to be normal again but it isn't. Tom began having trouble making simple decisions. He began isolating himself from family and friends and was plagued by nightmares and flashbacks, replaying the event in his mind over and over.

Tom needed help. When he finally went for therapy he was able to talk about everything he was going through. By recognising the symptoms he was told he was suffering from PTSD. That gave him some relief. With medication and therapy as well as learning breathing exercises for his panic attacks Tom began to recover. He had to learn to master the memory and revisit the trauma so that it became less overwhelming.

The rate of recovery from PTSD is high, particularly it if is recognised in good time. The field of research is still relatively new and statistics are giving experts a better understanding of how both body and mind react to trauma. Cognitive Behavioural Therapies (CBT) are also effective in relieving symptoms. These may include learning skills such a relaxation and guided self dialogue.

A relatively new approach is called 'eye movement desensitisation and reprocessing' (EMDR) which initially requires patients to fix their eyes upon the therapist's rapidly moving fingers and more latterly oscillating taps or tones while the patient concentrates on the traumatic event in the hope of becoming desensitised to it. So far research is finding a high success rate with this method.

There are also some very effective medications which can help sufferers of PTSD.

OBSESSIVE-COMPULSIVE DISORDER

DONALD'S STORY

Donald could be described as a gentle and sensitive child. When Donald was five he liked to put all his toys in a row on his bed before he went to sleep. This is normal as many children like order and routine in their lives. It helps them feel they have an element of control in a big world and they like some predictability so that they can sleep, secure in the knowledge that when they wake up their familiar toys will be there, exactly as they left them.

For Donald however it was a little different. He needed to have his mum in the room and the toys had to be precise or he would have to start again, and again, and again.

Donald lived with his mum and dad and sister in a big house. They went on expensive holidays and Donald always received lovely presents for Christmas and birthdays. Donald's dad worked for a large important company and earned lots of money. Some days dad worked on his computer at home. He was very bossy and quite scary and liked things done his way. He often lost his temper and sometimes mum cried. Donald loved his mum and dad very much and worked hard to be a good boy so daddy wouldn't be angry. Donald wanted things to be just right so that he had some control over a part of his life and that the big world which daddy and his big company represented wouldn't be angry with him. He would open and close drawers over and over and talk to himself. As he got older he would need his room in perfect order before he went to sleep. These rituals became a part of Donald's life.

Obsessive Compulsive behaviour is the result of an anxiety which has pervaded the mind, sometimes from as early as two or three years of age. Because a young mind is not sophisticated enough to deal with so much anxiety or in the way a child perceives them, there will be a disturbance in his normal development. Often then this person feels deeply insecure and needs to create protective structures in the form of compulsive rituals in order to have some control and thereby reduce anxiety. There is a tendency towards preciseness, orderliness and the insistence on rigid control. Obsessive Compulsive individuals often find it difficult to cope with unfamiliar situations.

One of the most common compulsions is hand washing which is done regularly and often, sometimes up to hundreds of time a day. This person is pre-occupied to an abnormal degree with danger from a certain source (obsession) and does what is needed to minimise this danger (compulsion). In the case of hand washing this person is afraid of germs and contamination from which, deep down, they feel they may die. Because these anxieties are often rooted in early childhood the solutions the unsophisticated mind of a child invents are unusual and immature. Being the adaptive animal we are, the adaptive and malleable brain adopts the behaviour making the damage difficult to undo. Once it then lodges in the automatic pilot part of the brain, the memory area for automatic response of learned behaviour such as walking, skipping or driving, etc. it feels normal. As adults they are aware the compulsion is irrational but because the brain has now adapted they are unable to control it.

The obsessive compulsive anxiety fixates on preventing some feared disaster. In Donald's case it was the fear of dad's anger which at some primitive level he feared might obliterate him. As his ego was not yet mature enough to cope with this danger his immature strategy was to make sure that he did what he could to prevent upsetting what was in his perception the all important dad. Another personality might have reacted differently but Donald protected himself and his precious mother in the only way he could.

A psychological understanding and Cognitive Behaviour Therapy (CBT) is often the most effective treatment for Obsessive Compulsive Disorder. Psychological insight into the reasons for their disorder and a *desensitisation programme* can help a person to deal with their problem. With professional help and a regulated programme of slow exposure and re-learning new habits they can begin recovery. For example, patients with hand washing compulsions were asked to stand at a sink but not allowed to wash. With the help of their therapist they then learned to talk through their feelings and, more importantly, their fears and gradually compulsions faded. For some, medications are helpful as well. Eventually, the new experience will change brain function.

PHOBIAS

To understand phobias we need to understand how the body responds to fear. In his book, the Human Mind (2003), Professor Robert Winston[17] neatly explains that fear takes two routes to the brain. The first travels lightning quick from our senses, eyes, ears and nose, and into various parts of the brain alerting our bodies to react immediately with a rush of adrenaline in order to make a quick escape. The second route has the fear stimuli travelling more slowly to the frontal cortex where our intellect and reason assesses it for real or perceived danger. Professor Winston uses the example of lying in his tent in the jungle when he suddenly sees something wriggling. He thinks it might be a snake and prepares for a quick exit but by now the slower route via his anterior temporal cortex has analysed it to be a piece of rope which moved as his sleeping bag pressed against it. He stops panicking. His pulse and breathing return to normal and blood sugar begins to fall. Normal blood flow return to his organs as he no longer has the need to prepare his body to rush into the blackness of the jungle or fight off lethal snakes .

Understanding these two routes of fear gives us a better idea of how phobias develop and how they can be treated. Our bodies naturally react to a fearful situation with a fight/flight mechanism. If something comes on us so quickly that our bodies do not have time to prepare for fight/flight then sometimes the event fuses in our brain and will make us fearful of the event indefinitely. We call that a phobia.

Phobias are irrational fears of perceived danger which can cause anxiety. Anxiety and fear are closely related, the difference being that anxiety comes from within us (perceived fear) and real fear comes from the outside world such as spiders, dogs, open spaces, enclosed spaces, etc. The sight of a spider may bring fear but the thought of a spider hurting you may bring on anxiety.

Therefore if a spider creates fear we need to know we can escape from it but anxiety is produced if we think we cannot escape.

SPECIFIC PHOBIA

A Phobia is an irrational fear of something. To be classified a phobia the fear must be persistent and intense, there must be a compelling need to flee or avoid the phobic object or situation and the fear must be irrational and not based on sound judgement. A phobia is a fear fused in the mind as a result of a threatening stimulus when it has not had a chance to prepare itself to deal with the object or situation.

Fear of lifts

A man gets mugged in a lift. He reports the incident and life goes on. Another man gets mugged in the same lift. From that day on this man can't set foot in a lift again. Depending on learned coping strategies and our personal temperament we all react differently. We naturally go to great lengths to avoid problems. We know it is sensible to be cautious. But if early learning caution has been overloaded with fear of consequence this could sow seeds for future anxiety.

Other emotions associated with anxiety are fear, worry and/or panic. These can manifest themselves in phobias, including agoraphobia, panic attacks, social phobias, post traumatic stress disorder, and obsessive compulsive disorder.

ARACHNOPHOBIA

Arachnophobia is a fear of spiders. To date, the most successful way of dealing with specific phobias is with speciality therapy such as Cognitive Behavioural Therapy. A CBT therapist will likely use a carefully constructed and monitored desensitisation programme. It involves exposing the individual in small doses to the source of their fear, i.e. a spider; by first letting the person see someone else handle the spider without fear and then slowly introducing the individual to the spider by getting closer in stages, and possibly handling it in the end.

AGORAPHOBIA

MARGARET'S STORY

Margaret hated going out. Since her husband died she found herself getting more and more anxious each time she went to the shops or to visit friends. As her husband had usually done the driving she felt frightened of travelling on her own. She started taking the bus but was anxious and always relieved to be home. Even walking to the shops was now becoming a terrifying experience and Margaret spent all of her time alone at home with a friend doing her shopping. By now the idea of leaving her flat threw her into a full blown panic attack.

Agoraphobia is one of the most common of phobias. It is an irrational fear of being in public places from which there is no escape. This results in the individual avoiding such public places, or crowds, busy streets, public transportation, lifts, tunnels, bridges, etc. Such places usually bring on panic attacks therefore the fear has become a fear of the places which may precipitate an attack.

As in other phobias, a gentle desensitisation programme would help Margaret slowly recover from her fear of going out.

SOCIAL PHOBIA

LUCY'S STORY

Lucy blushed and hated her blushing. At home she was often teased for blushing. It became a real problem when she was about twelve and in her maths class felt a now familiar blushing attack coming. She raised her hand, asked to go to the toilet and sat in the cubicle and blushed.

Life went on and Lucy tried to keep busy but whenever she had too much attention she blushed. At the table with her many brothers and sisters she would sit at the corner and if anyone laughed at her or put her on the spot she could easily escape and blush in private. Lucy was unaware she had a problem. She just felt better avoiding public situations or feeling exposed. She enjoyed her own company and spent much time reading. As an adult she enjoyed working with children who did not laugh at her or put her on the spot. Lucy enjoyed being a teacher but avoided the staff room. She preferred chatting with the children in the playground.

Lucy was a bright, sensitive and thoughtful child. She was the second youngest of six children. The youngest had a disability and needed a lot of attention. Lucy's father was 'old school' autocratic and a fearsome head of the household. The older children admired their father but the younger children feared him. Mother was kind and funny and clever but worked hard and had little time for Lucy as there was always much work with cooking and cleaning and minding little Leroy. When Lucy was a baby she would be handed from brother to sister to cot and spent much time not being held. Lucy would often rock herself in her cot. When she was six Lucy once overheard her father say that life was hard and that he wished the two youngest children had never been born. This did not make Lucy sad. She just felt she should not have been born.

Experts believe that without 'genuine interpersonal recognition' a human infant will fail to thrive. This means that in order to attain potentiality he needs at least the love and affection of one primary carer. They believe that psychological disturbance occurs when a person feels inferior and unworthy of an equal place amongst his or her fellows.[18]

In Lucy's case there are unconscious roots of feelings of unworthiness and inferiority. As she grew up her developing brain recorded this and adapted accordingly. Lucy believed others were more important then she was. In growing up father represented the outside world and Lucy became frightened of figures of authority. She worried that the important people would be angry with her and feel she should not be there.

A social phobia is a fear of social situations. A person with a social phobia will spend much time avoiding the feared circumstances. Often this person will force him or herself to endure the social or performance situation but experiences it with intense anxiety. They may also spend excessive amounts of time worrying about the anticipated event or social situation, such as a party or school social to excess. This puts a lot of strain on the body and can sometimes cause illness.

Social Phobia typically has an onset in the mid-teens, sometimes emerging out of a childhood history of social inhibition or shyness. Some individuals report an onset in early childhood. The course of social phobia is often continuous, and duration is usually life long. Common associated features of Social Phobia include hypersensitivity to criticism, negative evaluation or rejection, difficulty being assertive and low self-esteem with feelings of inferiority. The concern is that others will judge them harshly.

With help, Lucy can overcome her social phobia, so that she can have a normal life. For Lucy, counselling is the ideal solution. Lucy needs to engage with an adult on a one to one basis, so that she can feel of value to someone. For her the counsellor could be, to some extent, a parent substitute. She is then able, over time, to internalise the care and interest of an adult human being until she is ready to move on, carrying within her the care and unconditional support of the counsellor, like a parent. With this kind of help, and a desensitisation program exposing her in small doses to the feared situations Lucy may be helped to reduce her anxiety and improve her quality of life. She can then feel contained by her counsellor in stressful situations as might a child bravely going to the big school and mummy being proud of him. If Lucy has help to understand that she has equal value amongst her peers, it will eventually help her accept that she, like anyone, has social value.

Chapter Eleven
SEXUALITY AND GENDER ISSUES

HOMOSEXUALITY

We are all sexual beings. As nature seems to be fairly preoccupied with pro-creation and the preservation of the species it is widely accepted that conventional sexual behaviour involves sex between a male and a female in order to produce little males and females. We know this to be heterosexual behaviour as opposed to homosexual behaviour, which involves sex with same sex partners, and which is now fairly well accepted but which cannot produce offspring.

Homosexuality was considered a mental disorder, until in 1973 the American Psychiatric Association withdrew it from the Diagnostic Statistical Manual (DSM IV). As it was no longer a 'sexual disorder', large numbers of people were 'cured' overnight. Society now regards homosexuality as an orientation, a choice.

There has been found to date no biological reason for homosexuality. For decades many studies have been undertaken looking into hormonal, glandular, genetic or hereditary factors and none were found. Lawrence Hatterer,[19] American Psychiatrist maintains that 'homosexuals are not born but made' and Dr. Frank Lake[20] found much evidence relating early years' influences directly to homosexual orientation. Dr. Elizabeth Moberly,[21] psychologist and authority on homosexuality believes that it is essentially a state of incomplete (social) development or of unmet needs. She believes that "homosexual orientation is rooted in same-sex psychological deficiencies", that is, girls will have unresolved issues with mum and boys will have unresolved issues with dad, and arises from "difficulties in the parent child relationship, especially in the earlier years of life".

Although the media may lead us to believe that there are many gays in our society today, statistics tell us that less then 1.5% of the population in Britain is registered as co-habiting in an actively homosexual relationship.

As a modern society we categorise sexuality into acceptable groups. There are those with conventional sex drives, that is a male or female who makes advances towards the opposite sex in a socially acceptable way and eventually settles on one with whom he or she will co-habit and live happily ever after. Society will even tolerate Jack-the-lad who has an 'eye for the ladies' and accepts it is even okay for men to admire very young girls who are physically well developed from a respectable distance. Society frowns on predators who pursue women purely for their sexual gratification; it frowns on adulterers; and abhors child abusers.

Homosexuality seems to be tolerated as long as it's not 'in your face' or "hurting our children". Like anything, society eventually comes to terms with new ideas when they are presented slowly and is in the interest of the larger group. Television programs are wonderfully instrumental in educating the public in presenting such social issues as homosexual dilemmas in popular soap operas and endearing the public to the individuals involved. Thus we tolerate and may now embrace what might have been considered odd behaviour or an unusual choice. We are becoming desensitised to unfamiliar things such as two males kissing or two females making love.

So, what we call normal acceptable behaviour is forever changing but still fairly specific, and more to do with what the majority may regard as the natural order of things. Anyone with less normal inclinations will need to keep their deviancies to themselves or pursue these in secret with like-minded individuals.

WHY BE DIFFERENT?

So why are there so many people with non-heterosexual inclinations?

Well, let's face it. If you were on a desert island with only one other person, much as you hate to admit it, it probably wouldn't be long before you might seek physical comfort and possibly sexual gratification from that person regardless of who they were, male or female, young or old. In the dark and if it feels good and provides comfort, we'd likely go for it. A human's greatest attribute is his ability to adapt to his environment and thus it is not difficult to work out that we are all capable of homosexual relations. Sigmund Freud suggested that over a hundred years ago.

Some proof of that lies in what the experts call the 'plasticity' of the brain. The marvellous Professor Robert Winston, who is the reassuring face of many behaviour programs on the BBC tells us in his book 'the Human Mind' that before we are born our brain is developing at an explosive rate of 250,000 neurons per minute and from the moment we are born it starts to adapt itself to its environment. By the time a baby is one it has shed millions of unwanted neurons which are not needed in its environment and starts to adjust its development of neurons where they are needed. The very act of a stimulus encourages this growth so that if a baby sits on the floor and sees a brightly coloured ball some feet away it is the red ball that spurts the baby into action to want to possess it and boosts neuronal growth. It is the same with sexual development.

As sexuality develops it is adapting itself to its needs, so that if a baby feels warmth and comfort and receives milk from mother it begins to see femaleness as a good thing. If dad adds to that by bringing comfort to mother and baby, then baby will see maleness as a good thing. Once baby works out what sex he is at around the age of two, he will unconsciously work out that one day he may want to mate, and he will soon learn how to send out signals to attract a member of the opposite sex. We often see signs of coyness in little girls when they are around men, sometimes are early as age 2.

SEX ON HOLD

But now comes the really interesting bit. In his book, The Human Body which accompanied a major BBC television series presented by Professor Winston, Anthony Smith explains that if humans were like typical animals then we would be ready to start reproduction when we are four and stop growing when we are six. Instead "our bodies actively switch off sexual development" and waits approximately ten years before we become a sexual and reproductive being.[22] That's about the time we are at primary school and junior school and means that we have the benefit of developing our social selves as well as our physical and intellectual selves for a very long time before the onset of that very distracting part of our lives we call puberty. That makes us a very unique animal indeed. It certainly means there is no point in looking to the animal world for clues about normal behaviour. We are in a category all our own although it must be said that there is evidence of homosexual behaviour in the animal kingdom, according to David Attenborough's recent television series.

Baby knows its sex from around the age of two. Once it has accepted what sex he or she is, a child throws itself, so to speak, into their gender training for the foreseeable future. From this very early time we begin choosing our sexual orientation. Until we reach puberty and then adulthood many factors will still influence that choice.

One powerful factor is our identification with our same sex parent. It is that parent with whom we will identify, and that will reflect how we feel about our self, and our sexual identity. Our opposite sex parent will model for us how we will feel about the opposite sex, our reflective sexuality and our future partner.

It is fair to say that each human being starts with a mother and a father (even in a test tube, both a man and a woman have had to make a contribution) and that, in a conventional, nuclear family circumstance nature sends with the birth package a powerful set of instincts to nurture and protect that baby. Now baby has a conventional man and woman to model respective behaviour to him. Although life isn't always like that, we will start with that.

Even under these ideal conditions things can get tricky. After all, if a baby gets to choose, he needs to know what is on offer, and so needs exposure to both sexes. If the man or woman doesn't give him what he needs to thrive, that is, love and approval, then there will be what psychologists call 'interruptions to the normal development of behaviour'. The child will adapt himself accordingly, and in order to protect itself from pain he will steer his psychological and neurological self in a safe direction.

TWO REASONS FOR BEING GAY

There are two main reasons why a person chooses to be homosexual. One is because of an attraction to the same sex and the other because of an abhorrence of the opposite sex. The latter is easy to understand and if a child has suffered great physical or emotional pain as a result of offences caused by someone of the opposite sex he may seek comfort or sexual expression from what he or she considers a safer option. If a girl is constantly humiliated or sexually abused by father then she could go off men, big time. Alternatively, her esteem may become so low, she will choose abusive relationships. She could also unconsciously hate her mother for not protecting her and has to choose whom she hates the most to choose her sexuality. Not a nice premise. It is also difficult for boys. All circumstances vary and no two are the same, but if a boy gets constantly humiliated or sexually abused by father, he may react similarly. He may abhor men or he may choose homosexuality as now sex with males has become familiar ground.

The first reason however for why we may choose homosexuality, may be a bit more difficult to come to grips with. We know the adaptability of the human brain and that a baby or child will thrive if basic conditions are met for physical and mental growth. Any interruptions will cause problems and if there are interruptions in sexual development then things can go wrong. We learn our sexuality from our parents or primary carers. If a child doesn't properly bond with the same sex parent we have a psychological interruption. A child needs love and approval from mum and if that doesn't happen then a child cannot progress in that part of development. A girl child will continue to look for this until her need is met. If that doesn't happen then it may lay dormant for the ten or so years while sexuality goes underground and we get on with our socialising years until puberty. Then, at puberty our girl child with her unfulfilled needs may seek mother-love from other females to fulfil desires.

It is the same with unmet needs from the man in her life. If dad hasn't shown his precious baby girl the love and approval she needs she too may lay those feeling dormant until puberty and then look to males to fulfil her needs and become childlike and needy in her relationships. She may become promiscuous or the proverbial doormat to get the affection she so desperately needs. She will not be able to be a mature partner and will feel a deep unhappiness, unsure of why she is not fulfilled.

Boy children will have similar problems. If he doesn't get the love and approval he needs from mum, our lad may be the proverbial 'good boy' for his future wife and not be able to stand beside her as an equal partner. Or he may have resentments and carry these with him throughout his marriage. He may look to older women for a more mothering kind of relationship.

If unresolved needs apply to dad, then our boy too may lay these feelings dormant until puberty and his need for male love and approval may send him seeking relationships with members of his own sex. *This one is probably more common as fathers are often unavailable to their children, both physically, as traditionally they were out working, and emotionally as they often shied away from involvement in child care.* Boys often had few role models to emulate as their early world was heavily dominated by women, sometimes till secondary school. Many people may not understand why they are attracted to their own sex as they may either not remember their early relationships or may have blocked painful memories.

For healthy gender training boys need men to study. Girls are very lucky as they have their role models on hand from the moment they are born with mum and breast right there. They have mum's friends and playgroup leaders and teachers and dinner ladies to reinforce their training and unless their principal carer is quite harsh, they are generally fairly secure in their femaleness. Boys however are hard pressed to find role models and when they get to toddler group there is not a man in sight. An electrician comes in to fix the water heater and, at last, a man to study but he's soon gone and they are again left to flounder. Playgroup, school and still not a man in sight. The boys are now getting quite uncomfortable as they continuously have to take orders from women. Unconscious options then may include 'better switch off parts of the brain or adapt accordingly'.

If we reach adulthood with unresolved needs it becomes very difficult to recover from that. Not impossible but difficult. Counselling can help. At best we can try to understand ourselves and accept our limitations.

Alternatively, single sexed schools can promote homosexuality. If the only persons a child sees before and during puberty are members of his own sex and relationships are important, then sexuality can easily spill over into these relationships. A friend confided to me how it felt perfectly natural for her and her friends in an all-girl's school to have crushes on the older girls. This friend was married but admitted she would happily trade in her husband if a female relationship was offered to her.

Other reasons for choosing to be gay are familiar experiences in childhood or adolescence. In adulthood we like to re-create the comfort zones of our youth, and if there was much same sex activity in youth and these experiences brought pleasure then we will want to bring back some of that feel-good factor to compensate for the hard graft of adult life.

Self-talk can even do it. If a girl looks at herself in the mirror one day and decides she looks more like dad with a sturdy body, and nothing like mum with her delicate ways, she may feel nature has made a mistake and decide she ought to be male instead of a girly girl. She does, after all, much prefer working with dad in the garage and has spent many happy days there with him. At some level, mum and dad may agree and worse, collude with her and her choice. Without a word spoken a life altering decision may have been made. Had mum been more sturdily built and our youngster related to her same sex parent then things may have been completely different. If mum had recognised her daughter's insecurities, she may have talked to her about these and laid her fears of incongruity to rest.

Occasionally nature does make a mistake when there are problems with genital development but these cases are rare.

IT'S EVERYWHERE

Homosexuality is found in every known society. In fact, adolescent homosexuality was a common and accepted practice in ancient Athens and in the Mayan civilizations of Central America. Even today, it is not uncommon for groups of adolescent boys to engage in mutual masturbation when there is little else for them to do.

So, it is not surprising there is a high population of gay males in our society today. It is not so much that they are not interested in relationships with women but more to do with unresolved issues with same sex parents or opposite sex influences. They are then essentially 'stuck in the need' and cannot move on to a heterosexual relationship. Because we remember so little of our lives before age 4, many people are probably unaware but once the choice was made, at whatever age, the brain quickly adapts itself to the sexually preferred choice. Then mannerisms and interests soon change and become a part of their lives. Life is very hard for anyone in a minority group and I fear social stigma has caused our gay population a great deal of pain in making those choices.

My own personal view on sexuality is that I feel everyone needs a special friend or companion in their lives, regardless of their sexual orientation; someone to love, someone to care for and be cared by; that special face in a crowd; that special someone to choose a Christmas present for. It's nice to love and even nicer to be loved no matter what sex you are.

SEXUAL FETISHES

LOONERS

A 'looner' is a person with a fetish for balloons. He has little or no interest in sex with partners and prefers instead to spend his intimate time with balloons. He is a latex lover, turned on by the feel and smell of balloons and enjoys inflating them and rubbing against them. He finds high emotional drama in balloons expanding and potentially popping. He can only get excited by being with and fantasising about balloons. He may endlessly watch videos of balloons, and may lie and pretend to be in a conventional relationship in order to cover up his fetish.

MORE FETISHES

More common fetishes may include attaining sexual satisfaction from Voyeurism (peeping Tom), Exhibitionism, (exposing yourself to a stranger), Frotteurism (rubbing up against strangers in crowded places), Sexual Masochism (receiving pain and humiliation), Sexual Sadism, (causing pain and humiliation to others), Transvestism (cross dressing) and Paedophilia (gratification from pre-pubescent children). Because of the destructive nature of Paedophilia, it is included under Psychological disorders.

How does a fetish come about? To understand a fetish is to again see the marvellous adaptive process of the human mind and body. We all know that if ducklings hatch and their mother is not around that they attach themselves to the first moving thing they see. If that is your Wellington boot then the ducklings have imprinted in their brain that your boot is their mother. Good luck to you and your Wellington boot. It is somewhat the same with the mind and sexual adaptation.

If a person is highly aroused at some point in their early life and makes an association with whatever object happens to be around at that time, then by association that particular item will bring back the original highly aroused state each time it is around. We are an adaptive animal and once we have adapted ourselves to a particular way of being it becomes hard wired and it is a difficult thing to shift. So that if a child comes home from a party and mother sends him yet again up to his room so as not to be under her feet, and he becomes bored and stimulates himself sexually with his balloon from the party, then he will make a great association with the balloon and his sexual pleasure. If he spends a lot of time on his own, and in order to bring back the feeling in future times he will try that again, and eventually become attached to the item, sexually.

People with unusual sexual inclinations have similar adaptations and it is because of exciting, arousing experiences that they too have adopted behaviours which have brought pleasures in the past. These have found their way deep into their neurological development and experiential repertoire, so that it feels perfectly normal and can bring pleasure anytime they want.

Chapter Twelve

DEEP PSYCHOLOGICAL DISORDERS

This chapter is about psychological disorders, which are deeply rooted in our psyches. This is when things can go badly wrong. These are problems which can happen to people generally when they have needed to adapt themselves to behaviours to protect themselves from anxiety at a very early age, sometimes the age before memory.

Psychological Disorders

PERSONALITY DISORDER – PSYCHOSIS

TOMMY'S STORY

Tommy is 1, and lives with his single mum in a small flat above the newsagents. Tommy was often left alone when mummy went down to the shop to get cigarettes or alcohol. Mummy was drunk quite a lot and sometimes took drugs which made her hallucinate. Tommy loved his mum a lot and was happy when she hugged him tight and laughed out loud. Sometimes she laughed so loud that it would frighten him and he would cry. Sometimes she accidentally hurt him. Once she dropped him on the floor and she was so sorry she stroked him and stroked him until they both fell asleep. Life for Tommy was chaotic. There was no order in his life and no routine.

One day mummy came in and started throwing flowers from the vase around the room. She laughed and laughed so hard till she fell on the sofa and went to sleep. Tommy laughed too but mummy didn't get up. Tommy started to cry but mummy still didn't wake up. When Tommy finally stopped crying he sat on the floor. He played with the flowers and water puddles. He felt hungry and started to cry again. Mummy still didn't wake. He found some crisps and ate these and some beer in a tin. He felt unwell and cried again. Mummy still didn't wake up. Eventually

Tommy fell asleep on the floor. When he woke up in the dark he cried again. This time mummy woke up and didn't feel well. She shouted at Tommy. Tommy picked up some flowers and threw them hoping she would laugh but this time she didn't and became very angry, and hit him for making a mess.

Tommy has no safe space. Tommy has no reference points for sad or happy. Tommy has no sense of order. Tommy's life is chaotic and unsafe. If Tommy stays in this environment for an extended period of time Tommy's neurological development will be programmed badly and he will have problems when he grows up. A psychosis is a troubled and confused mind.

Tommy's story is a sad and disturbing one, and although fictitious, it is a life we know many children endure in many corners of the globe. It is not difficult to see how hard it is for Tommy to survive such a lifestyle. Many of these children grow up with self-loathing and become self-harmers as they know that things aren't right and they blame themselves. They find it difficult to make sense of things. They can't blame their parents because they need them. By the time they reach school age they have learned much anti-social behaviour and have been told so often how worthless they are they now believe it. They are at the mercy of their programmers, their primary carers.

Because everyone is different and everyone's circumstances vary there are endless different anti-social behaviours and clinicians do have a difficult time categorising these in order to procure treatment.

Too Much Damage

Let's see how Tommy is getting on. As he grows up and whenever mummy gets frustrated or Tommy cried she would take her frustrations out on Tommy and hit him hard and often. Then after a few drinks she would be sorry and stroke him and caress him and kiss him and say how sorry she was. Mummy could be so sweet and kind. After a while Tommy didn't mind being hit anymore because he knew that afterwards he would get stroked and loved. Eventually he started to look forward to the abuse because it became part of the ritual which brought the comfort he so desperately needed. If he started to welcome the violence it is then not difficult to understand where some forms of masochism may have its roots and in adulthood one may welcome pain if it was followed by pleasure.

A psyche can adapt and protect itself from a lot but not deep rooted damage. Just as the body can protect itself from many viruses, bacteria, cuts and abrasions with its automatic healing process, it has its limits and cannot cope with deep trauma such as an amputation or organ failure, etc. Without medical intervention such persons would die. So too, the psychological brain is very resilient and can protect itself well, but not from deep psychological damage. Nature, therefore, places a child in the hands of two adults who need to protect him from harm. Psychotic behaviour is the result of abusing the adaptive process.

SCHIZOPHRENIA

HARRY'S STORY

Harry's household was chaotic with many sisters who were much older then he was. Mother never wanted him and didn't even like boys. He was often locked in his room and even more often left outside in the garden. Mother made it clear that he was unwelcome. His sisters took their cue from mother and treated him the same. Life was hard enough for them with mother's temper and absurd rules.

Harry couldn't remember the first time he saw flashes in his head. It may have been when mother was shouting at one of his sisters yet again. He dared not speak but the rage in him felt like it was going to burst out. He began hallucinating and couldn't make sense of the madness going on his head. These got worse as the anger inside him bubbled out of control. To survive he learned to ignore his rage and push away feelings of fear and anger.

Life was tough for Harry. He often got into trouble at school and spent much time in and out of borstal. When he was in his early 20's Harry started to hear voices in his head which began controlling his life. He then spent much time in and out of psychiatric units.

Harry is a damaged boy. Harry did not have an upbringing conducive to becoming mentally healthy. He felt emotions he could not make sense of when he was too young. He had no father for gender training. He had no love or affection to give him a sense of self esteem. He had no reference points for good or bad behaviour. He had few if any good memories as a foundation to build his future on.

Experts believe that human infants fail to thrive in the absence of genuine interpersonal recognition. That means a child cannot thrive without at least the love and affection of its mother or carer. They believe that psychological disturbance occurs when an individual feels inferior and unworthy of an equal place amongst his or her fellows.

We are social animals and have an innate need to belong, and with strong feelings of inferiority a person's potentiality cannot grow.

For a time Harry lost himself in alcohol. He died at an early age of organ failure.

SELF HARMING

CLAIRE'S STORY

Claire was a mum who regularly self harmed. She knew it was wrong but still felt compelled to cut her arms when she could no longer cope. She tried hard to resist the compulsion. It had been over a year since she last hurt herself this way but this time she felt a strong urge. Her eyes kept darting towards the window sill where the knives stood in their block. Once or twice she took out the smallest but sharpest one and then replaced it. She moved the block out of sight and went out. When she came back, she put the groceries away, took out the small sharp knife and cut herself. It had been unbearable. She knew if she hadn't released that tension she would have started shouting and abusing her children as soon as they got home from school. Claire felt a momentary release of a deep pain inside.

When Claire was born her mother suffered from depression. Claire's mother spent much time in and out of psychiatric wards and when she was home she mostly neglected Claire. As Claire grew and began to toddle she craved to be held by her mother and for her mum to pay attention to her. Mother was vacant and self-absorbed. Claire believed that mum neglected her because she didn't deserve to be loved. Claire felt unlovable.

It is difficult to understand why anyone would self-harm and to most such behaviour would seem shocking, maybe frightening and certainly socially unacceptable. But in reality it is not so different from other forms of self harm which we see as more socially acceptable. For example, activities which may be described as more 'normal' ways of self harming are over-working, heavy smoking, drinking alcohol, over eating and even to some extend extreme sport. We know these are ways we harm our bodies but they bring emotional relief. It then brings this behaviour into a dimension with which we can more easily relate.

In an interview discussing self harm, psychotherapist Maggie Turp says that we all have a capacity for self-care and we believe that psychological disturbance can affect that. She argues that according to psychoanalytic theory that this is mainly due to "parenting in the first two years of life, and the availability or unavailability of a good internal object". This means that a good carer will reflect goodness for baby to internalise and who will then have the experience of feeling good about himself as well as his carer who represents the outside world. She says "babies are born totally dependent; they do not know how to self soothe and the kind of care they receive at this point forms the basis of their own care of themselves later in life". She adds, "If you haven't had the experience of being soothed at a young age, you might find yourself resorting to quite desperate measures to calm yourself down as an adult."[23]

Psychotherapy can eventually help a self-harmer to come to terms with their compulsions.

PAEDOPHILIA – FETISHISM

JACK'S STORY

It had been Jack's first camping trip when his scout leader, Tim asked him to climb into his sleeping bag with him and placed the boy's hands on his genitals.

Jack was 11 when they moved to the small village in the midlands from London. Dad was away a lot so Jack's mum took him to his first scout meeting. Jack loved it. He was very excited to tell mum about Tim the scout leader who would take them camping this summer. Jack couldn't wait. He had never been camping before.

He really liked Tim who spent extra time with him so that he could catch up on work he had missed out on from the first term. They had even shared secrets together. He had been a little uncomfortable when Tim had stared at him in the showers but had soon forgotten that.

Now he didn't know what to do. He had six more nights at camp and he just wanted to go home and sleep in his own bed. He knew he couldn't tell a soul.

Paedophilia is an illness. Molesting a child is a crime. Most parents worry about strangers abducting or hurting their child but statistics now tell us that the majority of offenders are people in the family or community that they have trusted. They can be a teacher, coach, religious leader, scout leader and even a family member such as an uncle or parent.

Such individuals are clever. They easily spot potential victims and will carefully begin grooming them over time so that the child feels collusive. They will involve the child to believe that somehow they wanted this to happen. Pleasurable feelings from stimulation confuse him further as the child gets drawn into the offender's pathological trap.

Jack's life changed that first day of camp. From that day on he became insular, sad, and damaged. For the rest of his life now Jack will feel tarnished. It will be difficult for Jack to embrace his future with a normal and healthy anticipation. Future relationships will be difficult. His esteem will suffer drastically. His lovely life is essentially spoiled. He will get through it but not happily. Many boys like this will carry that tarnish and shame for the rest of their lives.

With help, however, that can be minimized and the sooner it is dealt with the sooner the damage can be reduced and healing can start. There is much support around today to help victims of abuse.

GENERAL PERSONALITY DISORDER

AMY'S STORY
Amy's mother suffered from mood swings. She was often depressed and also lost her temper with the children. Amy was 2½ and didn't understand about depression. She knew mummy was often sad and sometimes quite cross. She knew mummy shouted at them quite a lot. Amy would lie in bed and hear mummy crying and shouting at Daddy and as she fell asleep the shouting sometimes became part of her dream. It felt like the anxiety would sleep with her. Amy felt confused and wanted mummy to hold her. Whenever she cried and needed a cuddle her mummy would get angry and sometimes hit Amy. Often when dad came home and heard about the crying he would hit Amy. Once they were in a shop and when Amy cried her mother lost it and dad ended up dragging Amy home and locking her in a cupboard.

As Amy grew up she felt different from her friends. She tried to hide in dark oversized clothes and wore lots of dark make-up so Amy herself wouldn't be seen. She hated evenings and felt deep unexplained fears. In order to cover up these horrible feelings, Amy had discovered that some drugs made her feel better, and soon eased herself into a world of drugs and the people who used them.

From the time she was born Amy was cared for by a depressed mum. She wasn't always picked up when it was needed or fed when she was hungry. She wasn't always cuddled when she was frightened, angry or sad and was often beaten when she felt sad and confused. There was no one around to be proud of Amy when she took her first steps a few days after her first birthday.

Because there are a myriad of different circumstances in the bringing up of even a greater number of different personalities there are many things that can go wrong. This is why there are many, many different disorders and sometimes things can go badly wrong.

Personality disorder is a broad term which can include more serious disorders such as anti-social personality disorder which can be as a result of psychological disturbances or interruptions in the normal development of a child during the very early years. Personality Disorder is when a child has been denied, very early on in life, the encouragement and physical touch she needs to cope in a complicated world. Instead Amy lived in an atmosphere of confusion, neglect, and punishment. She felt she was often punished for being a child.

Amy's adaptive processes have been so totally confused she has no idea what is real and what isn't. Because her mind had no safe space, it moves in and out of states of surreal existence, seeking comfort where she could. She has few if any reference points by which to judge reality.

By the time Amy went to school her life became more normal but Amy never recovered from the damaging effects of the abuse during her early years. An unsettledness invaded Amy's life in her late teens and life became very difficult for Amy.

ANTI SOCIAL PERSONALITY DISORDER, (FORMERLY PSYCHOPATHY)

Anti-social personality disorder sounds fairly inoffensive but it is probably the most serious of social disorders. Formerly called Psychopathy, it results from too much disruption in the normal development of the mind so that damage is virtually irreparable.

JAMIE'S STORY

When Jamie was two he was put into care, and spent the next ten years in and out of care homes and was eventually confined in a secure group home. Jamie was a lively character and maybe if he had been raised in a loving home he may have put all that energy to more constructive use. As it was Jamie was always in trouble. When he was born his sixteen year old mum found him an imposition and his nineteen year old dad felt the best way to stop him crying was to hit him. By the time he was two he was removed from his parents and placed in a home where he was mostly left in his cot with little human contact. Because of his lively character Jamie amused himself as best he could and let his presence be known by making lots of noise, breaking things and making himself very unpopular with his carers, who tried to control him with anger and abuse. They eventually moved Jamie on and on and on. As no one cared for Jamie, it is not hard to see that Jamie never learned about caring.

Unbeknown to Jamie at the time, the human psyche needs the love and affection of a mother or carer in order to thrive and that neurological development adapts the brain to its early programming. If there is an absence of care the brain develops accordingly.

Babies rely on others to take care of them. Babies also instinctively know they each need the love of a carer and then if he doesn't get it experts in the psychoanalytic field believe baby registers deep anger. Unresolved anger goes inwards and may turn into depression. Because Jamie was far too young to deal with these strong emotions the psyche protects itself by burying these deeply.

Whenever Jamie got the chance he ran away from where he was living. He got pleasure from breaking rules and dodging the system. He stole money to get what he needed and enjoyed the stealing as much as the spending. It made him feel alive.

One day Jamie spotted an elderly lady in the park and as usual ran along and snatched her bag, however, the old woman clung tight. Jamie pulled harder but she shouted abuse at him. An excitement came over Jamie and he felt a deep untapped rage. He hit her and laughed. She shouted more abuse and the more she did the more thrilling Jamie found it to hit, punch and kick her. At last she went quiet but Jamie kept kicking and laughing.

Persons with Antisocial Personality Disorder often lack empathy and tend to be callous, cynical and contemptuous of the feelings, rights and sufferings of others. They may have an inflated and arrogant self appraisal and believe that ordinary work is beneath them. They may have an unrealistic view of themselves and their future. They may be excessively opinionated, self assured and cocky.

Much research has been done over the years to give clues to anti-social personality disorder and possible contributors to it. In a study, 870 children who exhibited antisocial behaviour[24] were interviewed later as adults. "Those who showed antisocial personality disorder as adults had poor parental discipline as children, either inconsistent discipline or lack of discipline. They also tended to have a father who showed anti-social behaviour."

In neurological development, under normal circumstances, the sensory areas mature during early childhood. The limbic system which houses our emotions is in place by puberty and by the time we reach our late teens we have the maturing of our frontal lobes which means we can now more readily control our emotions. Understanding and considered response develop by late adolescence. The brain is not fully formed until we reach our early twenties. It is a gradual learning process and it stands to reason that where there is no solid foundation there can be no solid structure. If emotions aren't required then the brain adapts itself by pruning. Jamie's lively character might have served him better had it been nurtured with love and care. Instead it was replaced by anger and hostility. There is now deep psychological disturbance. His little brain adapted accordingly. It is then not surprising that Jamie feels little concern for society and has not developed what we call a 'social conscience'.

Only intensive psychotherapy and a systematic emotional relearning can save Jamie now. Prison is probably the best he can hope for.

References

[1] Anthony Smith, 1998, *The Human Body*, pp.62–3, BBC Books.

[2] Sigmund Freud, 1923, *The Ego and the ID*.

[3] Robert Winston, 2003, *The Human Mind* , p.51, Bantam Press.

[4] Anthony Smith, 1998, *The Human Body*,p.72, BBC Books.

[5] Robert Winston, 2003, *The Human Mind*, p.156,Bantam Press.

[6] Abraham Maslow, 1970, *Transpersonal Psychology – Hierarchy of Needs*, Viking, New York.

[7] M. Eysenck, 1998, Psychology Textbook, Schachterer 1971.

[8] "Our Deepest Fear", poem, written by Marianne Williamson (heavily rumoured to be Nelson Mandela).

[9] Dr. Phil McGraw(American Psychologist and TV Presenter, 2000, *Relationship Rescue*, Vermillion.

[10] Windy Dryden, 1996, *Handbook of Individual Therapy*, p109, Sage Publications.

[11] A Lemma, 1996, *Introduction to Psychopathology*, Sage Publications.

[12] A Lemma, 1996, *Introduction to Psychopathology*, Sage Publications.

[13] A Lemma, 1996, *Introduction to Psychopathology*, Sage Publications.

[14] A Lemma, 1996, *Introduction to Psychopathology*, Sage Publications.

[15] Prader-Willi disorder, 1956, Andrea Prada and Heinrich Willi.

[16] Department of Clinical Psychology, *Defeating Depression*, West Berkshire NHS Trust.

[17] Robert Winston, 2003, *The Human Mind*, p.156, Bantam Press

[18] Maggie Turp, 2002, *Hidden Self Harm*, Jessica Kingsley.

[19] Lawrence Hatterer, 1998, *Homosexuality*, Vol.23, Craig Donnelan.

[20] Elizabeth Moberly, 1983, *Homosexuality*, James Clarke & Co.

[21] Frank Lake, 1992, *Maternal-Fetal Distress-Syndrome, An Analysis.*

[22] Anthony Smith, 1998, *The Human Body*, p.89, BBC Books.

[23] Windy Dryden, 1996, Handbook of Individual Therapy, p.226, Sage Publications.

[24] Daniel Goleman, 1990, *Emotional Intelligence*, p.196, Bantam Press.

Ingram Content Group UK Ltd.
Milton Keynes UK
UKHW011427060323
418105UK00017B/1704